HOW TO WRITE A GREAT RESEARCH PAPER

A Step-By-Step Guide

by Leland Graham and Darriel Ledbetter

Incentive Publications, Inc.
Nashville, Tennessee

ACKNOWLEDGEMENTS

The authors would like to gratefully acknowledge the assistance and suggestions of the following people:

Eirik Anderson, Katherine Bates, Wendy Bohanon,
Tonya Collins, Harriett Cook, Keith Cooley,
Charlotte Darnell, Monica Harden, Janet Jordan,
Sue Kennedy, Frank Loftis, Frankie Long,
Jeremy Mooney, Jamie NeSmith, Heather Rushing,
Dianne Selman, Angel Shumate, Claudette Smith,
John Spilane, Trina Sularin, Kerry Walker,
and Jeanna Williams

Cover and Illustrations by Geoffrey Brittingham
Edited by Leslie Britt

ISBN 0-86530-252-9

1   2   3   4   5   6   7   8   9   10   07   06   05   04

PRINTED IN THE UNITED STATES OF AMERICA
www.incentivepublications.com

Table of Contents

INTRODUCTION

The research paper is quite likely to be an intimidating assignment to the middle school student because of its length (it is typically 500 words or more) and the fact that it contains research and, therefore, does not spring primarily from the student's imagination. Writing the research paper is not a mere test of a student's creative ability, but a test of his or her ability to search out, recognize, accumulate, organize, and interpret a set of facts on a given topic. In fact, perhaps the chief goal of the research paper is to teach the student how to obtain needed information from the library.

This book was designed to walk the student step-by-step through the process of writing the research paper. Its main objectives are to make the research paper seem less intimidating and to provide the student with an understanding of the process of writing the research paper from the outset of the project. Each chapter covers a different step in the process and is written in friendly language with plenty of specific examples. Reproducible worksheets provide students with practice in completing each step. In addition to the twelve student chapters and conclusion, a section just for teachers has been included in the back of the book. This section contains suggested research paper topics, a reproducible letter to introduce the research paper to parents, tips on student oral presentations based on their research papers, and a certificate of research.

The research paper style introduced in this manual is based on the one suggested by the MLA (Modern Language Association) style manual. However, it is important to note that there are other styles which may be introduced and that no one of them is more "correct" than any other. The main point to stress to your students is that the style they adopt for their papers be consistent, easy for them to use, and easy for the reader to understand.

It is hoped that this manual will make teaching the research paper less complicated for you, the teacher, and understanding the research paper process easier for your students.

Chapter One

CHOOSING THE TOPIC AND GETTING ORGANIZED

What Is A Research Paper?

A research paper is an investigative, written report based upon information compiled from a variety of resources. (Your school or local library will contain most of the resources and materials you will need for the research paper, such as encyclopedias, dictionaries, periodicals or magazines, newspapers, vertical files, and a host of other reference books.) Most teachers who assign research papers are concerned not only with the finished product but also with the process involved in obtaining the information. It is this process which will be introduced and examined in this guide. Students who follow a step-by-step process in writing the research paper will always discover much more than initially anticipated.

If you want to write a successful research paper, follow these steps:

1. If the teacher allows you, select a topic that you find interesting.
2. Always observe your teacher's guidelines.
3. Since a research paper is usually an ongoing process (at least six weeks), schedule your time wisely and work steadily every day.

What Do You Think?

If you follow the steps outlined in this book, you will find writing a research paper to be an easy and rewarding task. Prior to beginning work on the paper, organize your materials in a folder. Since many teachers require all working materials to be submitted at the end of the research period, this folder will serve as an easy reference for the project as well as for future assignments on this topic.

Choosing The Topic

An important part of choosing a topic for a research paper is selecting one that is interesting to you—a subject about which you have always wanted to learn more or an adventure into an entirely new realm of study. Students sometimes are tempted to describe and narrate their personal experiences (for example, "a week at the beach" or "your life as a younger sister or brother") for their research paper. However, it must be remembered that a research paper is an investigative report based on facts or theories. It is possible to write a factual paper on a subject in which you are genuinely interested. For example, you may write your research paper on dinosaurs and incorporate information from the movie *Jurassic Park*.

In selecting a topic, your teacher may identify the broad (or general) subject for your research paper. It will then be up to you to find a specific (or narrower) subtopic to research. For example, if your teacher has assigned you to write a research paper on the topic of dinosaurs, a general subject, your task is to divide this general subject into specific, more narrow subtopics. You might begin the task of identifying subtopics by asking questions about your topic such as these:
- How would you describe the vegetation during the time of the dinosaurs?
- How would you describe the climate during this era?
- How are dinosaurs classified in the animal kingdom?
- What are some physical characteristics of dinosaurs?

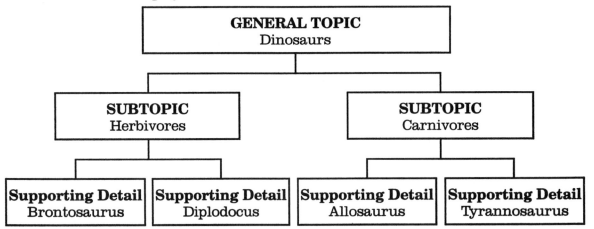

What Do You Think?

Before you begin to write, choose a topic from a range of areas and independently browse, brainstorm, question, predict, and focus on the research process. Before you make a final decision about your subject, check the library to review the types of sources available on this topic. A qualified paper usually needs at least two books, two articles from periodicals, and one article from an encyclopedia. If your topic is relatively new or technical, you may not find all of the information you need to document your paper.

CHOOSING THE TOPIC

Activity One

Some of the following topics are acceptable for a factual paper; others are not. On your paper, write **A** for topics that are acceptable (specific topics) and **U** for those that are unacceptable (too broad). You should be able to explain your responses.

____ 1. The role of the American woman in modern politics

____ 2. Recycling

____ 3. Shakespeare and his love poetry

____ 4. The migration of Hispanics into the southern United States

____ 5. Space explorations

____ 6. The history of chewing gum

____ 7. The decline of rain forests and its relationship to climate change

____ 8. The influence of African-Americans in American literature

Activity Two

Before you begin writing your research paper, you must select an appropriate topic. To help you select an appropriate topic, answer the following questions as you fill in the pyramid below with your own topics, subtopics, and supporting details. Begin by choosing a general topic that interests you. Then, fill in the rest of the boxes with specific subtopics and supporting details.

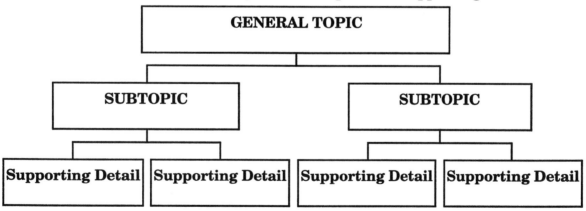

1. How long is my paper supposed to be? (I must make sure that my topic is limited enough to be covered thoroughly.)

2. Do I like my chosen subject? Which features of the general subject interest me the most?

3. Have I checked to make sure that there is enough available information? (If you have chosen a very narrow topic, such as "The Special Effects In *Jurassic Park*," you might not find enough facts or information for a lengthy paper.)

Name_____   Date _____

CHOOSING THE TOPIC, Page 2

Activity Three

When you are given the opportunity to select your topic (some teachers may choose to let you select from a list of topics), choose your subject from a general area, such as "Learning to Speak a Foreign Language." Then begin to think of a specific category related to your topic. For example, if the area you selected is "Learning to Speak a Foreign Language," your subject might be "Learning to Speak Spanish." Look at the areas below. Then write a subject for each that might be of interest to you if you were writing a research paper. Finally, circle the one that would interest you the most.

AREAS	SUBJECTS
Foreign Languages	Spanish
Science Experiments	
Native Americans	
Music	
Natural Disasters	
Horror Movies	
Space Explorations	
Computers	

Activity Four

Now that you have selected your subject, your next step is to search for a variety of resources. Use any of the following: encyclopedias, dictionaries, newspapers, magazines, almanacs, and books listed in the card catalog. Be sure there are enough sources for you to use. In the spaces provided, write at least six resources that you find on your subject.

SUBJECT: _____	
RESOURCES	**PAGE OR VOLUME**
1.	
2.	
3.	
4.	
5.	
6.	

*Name*_____   *Date* _____

The Dewey Decimal System

Your library will classify its books by either the Dewey Decimal System or the Library of Congress System. More than likely your school library will use the Dewey Decimal System, which was developed by Melvil Dewey, an American librarian. Under the Dewey Decimal System, books are classified under ten headings:

000-099   **General Works** (encyclopedias, reference materials)

100-199   **Philosophy** (ethics, psychology)

200-299   **Religion** (Christian theology, Bible, natural theology)

300-399   **Social Sciences** (economics, government, education)

400-499   **Language** (English, German, French, Italian, Spanish, Latin, other languages, dictionaries, grammar)

500-599   **Natural Sciences and Mathematics** (mathematics, astronomy, biology, physics, chemistry, earth science, botany)

600-699   **Technology** (medical sciences, engineering, agriculture, management, manufacturing)

700-799   **The Arts** (architecture, sculpture, painting, music, photography, printing, recreational and performing arts)

800-899   **Literature and Rhetoric** (poetry, plays, classics, and novels from all over the world)

900-999   **Geography and History** (geography, travel, ancient history, general history of the continents)

Activity:

Read the title of each book listed below. Then determine in which classification of the Dewey Decimal System it belongs. Write your answers in the spaces provided.

_____ Complete Book of Sports Medicine   _____ The Life of Christ

_____ The Last of the Mohicans   _____ World Book Encyclopedia

_____ The Psychology of Sigmund Freud   _____ The Peaceable Kingdom

_____ Webster's New English Dictionary   _____ Environmental Careers

_____ Plants That Changed the World   _____ How To Draw Cartoons

_____ Pictorial History of Black America   _____ The Mysterious Earth

_____ Rise and Fall of the Roman Empire   _____ Famous First Facts

_____ Incredible Structures   _____ Acts and Facts

Name_____   Date _____

Learning To Use
The Card Catalog

It is not necessary to remember the headings of the Dewey Decimal System in order to find a book in your library. Every book in the library has a Dewey Decimal System number all its own. The number appears in the upper left corner of any one of several cards arranged in a cabinet called the *card catalog*. (if your library is computerized you will have an electronic catalog). This number is the *call number*. Beneath the call number is the first letter of the author's last name. The card catalog, arranged alphabetically, contains at least three cards for each book: an *author card*, a *title card*, and a *subject card*.

Author Card

Look up the author card if you are seeking a book by a particular author but do not know the name of the book. On the author card, the author's name appears at the top of the card with the title of the book immediately below it. There will be a different author card for each title by the same author. Author cards with the same author are arranged according to the alphabetical order of the book titles.

Title Card

If you know the title of the book but not the author's name, refer to the title card. The title of the book appears at the top of the card directly followed by the author's name. Remember: If the first word of the title is "A," "An," or "The," the card is filed alphabetically according to the second word in the title of the book.

Subject Card

In the event that you do not have a specific book in mind, but are looking for information on a certain topic, you would look for the subject card. The subject of the book is what appears first on the subject card. Like the author cards and title cards, the subject cards are organized alphabetically in the card catalog.

Study These Sample Cards

```
292     Witting, Alisoun
W       A treasury of Greek mythology;
        illus. by James Barry.  Harvey
        [c1965]
        125p illus (part col)

        A collection of Greek myths including the
        stories of Icarus, Persephone, Theseus, and
        Ariadne.
        Bibliog

        1 Mythology, Classical  I Illus
        II  T


03847    14        559602                 8291
```
Author Card

```
        A treasury of Greek mythology

292     Witting, Alisoun
W       A treasury of Greek mythology;
        illus. by James Barry.  Harvey
        [c1965]
        125p illus (part col)
        A collection of Greek myths including the
        stories of Icarus, Persephone, Theseus, and
        Ariadne.
        Bibliog

        1 Mythology, Classical  I Illus
        II  T
47       14        559602                 8291
```
Title Card

```
        MYTHOLOGY, CLASSICAL

292     Witting, Alisoun
W       A treasury of Greek mythology;
        illus. by James Barry.  Harvey
        [c1965]
        125p illus (part col)
        A collection of Greek myths including the
        stories of Icarus, Persephone, Theseus, and
        Ariadne.
        Bibliog
        1 Mythology, Classical  I Illus
        II  T


03847    14        559602                 8291
```
Subject Card

15

The Card Catalog

Activity One

Using the card catalog (or electronic card catalog) in your school library, list the call number, title, author, and date of publication of at least one book on each of the following subjects:

1. Football
2. South America
3. Greek Myths
4. Moon
5. Music
6. Dances
7. Space Exploration
8. American Poets and Poetry
9. Native Americans
10. Martin Luther King, Jr.

Activity Two

Pretend that you are writing a research paper on dinosaurs. Decide which card listed below is the author card, title card, and subject card. Record your answers in the blank spaces provided.

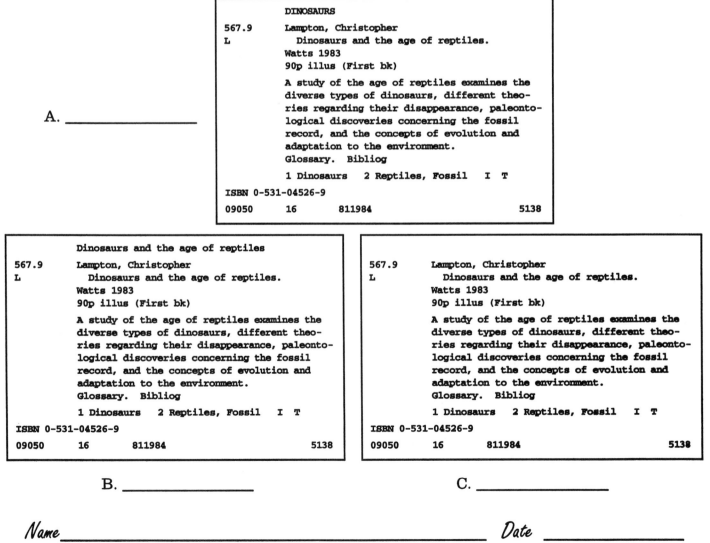

```
              DINOSAURS
    567.9     Lampton, Christopher
    L             Dinosaurs and the age of reptiles.
              Watts 1983
              90p illus (First bk)

              A study of the age of reptiles examines the
              diverse types of dinosaurs, different theo-
              ries regarding their disappearance, paleonto-
              logical discoveries concerning the fossil
              record, and the concepts of evolution and
              adaptation to the environment.
              Glossary.  Bibliog

              1 Dinosaurs    2 Reptiles, Fossil    I  T
    ISBN 0-531-04526-9
    09050      16      811984                    5138
```

A. _____

```
              Dinosaurs and the age of reptiles
    567.9     Lampton, Christopher
    L             Dinosaurs and the age of reptiles.
              Watts 1983
              90p illus (First bk)

              A study of the age of reptiles examines the
              diverse types of dinosaurs, different theo-
              ries regarding their disappearance, paleonto-
              logical discoveries concerning the fossil
              record, and the concepts of evolution and
              adaptation to the environment.
              Glossary.  Bibliog

              1 Dinosaurs    2 Reptiles, Fossil    I  T
    ISBN 0-531-04526-9
    09050      16      811984                    5138
```

B. _____

```
    567.9     Lampton, Christopher
    L             Dinosaurs and the age of reptiles.
              Watts 1983
              90p illus (First bk)

              A study of the age of reptiles examines the
              diverse types of dinosaurs, different theo-
              ries regarding their disappearance, paleonto-
              logical discoveries concerning the fossil
              record, and the concepts of evolution and
              adaptation to the environment.
              Glossary.  Bibliog

              1 Dinosaurs    2 Reptiles, Fossil    I  T
    ISBN 0-531-04526-9
    09050      16      811984                    5138
```

C. _____

Name_____ Date _____

MONTHLY PLANNER: It is important that you plan your research paper properly. Use this monthly planner to record all the deadline dates for each step in the process of writing your paper. Then decide how much time each week you want to allot for completing each step.

MONTH OF

SUNDAY	MONDAY	TUESDAY	WEDNESDAY	THURSDAY	FRIDAY	SATURDAY

Research Paper Progress Checklist

To write your research paper and track your progress, you will need to follow these steps in order. Staple this progress checklist inside the front cover of your research folder.

Steps	Date Assigned	Date Due	Completed
1. Choosing the Topic			
2. Selecting the Resources			
3. Writing the Bibliography Cards			
4. Taking Notes on the Facts			
5. Writing the Preliminary Outline			
6. Writing the First Draft			
7. Writing the Final Outline			
8. Writing the Final Draft			
9. Preparing the Final Bibliography			
10. Writing the Final Paper			
11. Completing the Finishing Touches			

Name _____ Date _____

Chapter Two

SELECTING THE RESOURCES AND MATERIALS

Learning to use resources and materials from the reference section of the library is a valuable aid for writing the research paper. The reference section of the library contains a wide variety of useful reference materials. Some resource materials are encyclopedias, dictionaries, *the Readers' Guide to Periodical Literature,* atlases, almanacs, and the vertical file. There are, of course, many more. These materials, however, cannot be checked out— they may be used only in the library. Although you may not check out reference materials, most libraries allow you to make photocopies of the information you read.

The Student

The most important resource available to you is you! Sometimes, both the teacher and the student forget that the student is a real, living source of information, with a wide variety of experiences to share. You are living in the world as a thinking and feeling creature. Hopefully, the teacher will allow you to use your experiences in writing your paper, regardless of the research topic.

The Librarian/Media Specialist

The next important resource available to you is your school's librarian or media specialist. This person is a virtual "walking encyclopedia" of information, just waiting to answer your questions and help you in any way. In addition, the librarian knows the location of the resources in the library, understands how to use the computers, and suggests ways to find quick, reliable information. Do not hesitate to make use of this wonderful resource.

Encyclopedias

There are many different sets of encyclopedias, so take time to browse through and become acquainted with all of them. An encyclopedia offers a variety of articles (usually brief) on many different subjects. Some encyclopedias you are likely to find in your library are *Britannica Junior, Collier's, Compton's, Compton's Pictured, Grolier's,* and *World Book.* When starting your research, it is a good idea to check the encyclopedia first for a "bird's-eye view" of your subject before moving on to more detailed sources. For example, if you are doing a research paper on how Mark Twain's life affected the subject matter in *The Adventures of Tom Sawyer,* you will look up Twain in the encyclopedia to get an overall view before checking the other references.

DICTIONARIES

The most commonly used dictionary in the library is the *Oxford English Dictionary* (OED), which provides easy reference to spelling, syllabication, word origin, parts of speech, as well as definition. Another commonly used dictionary is the biographical dictionary, which supplies information about famous people's lives. Some common biographical dictionaries include *Twentieth Century Authors, Who's Who in America,* and *Webster's Biographical Dictionary.*

READERS' GUIDE TO PERIODICAL LITERATURE

In order to find a particular magazine article on a specific subject, the library has a distinctive reference book entitled the *Readers' Guide to Periodical Literature.* The *Readers' Guide,* which is comprised of more than one hundred magazines, indexes articles by author and subject.

ATLASES

If you are a student who enjoys learning about different cities and countries of the world, then you will want to learn to use the atlas. There are many types of atlases, but they all share some similarities. Some people think of an atlas as only a book of maps, but it is much more. An atlas contains information and facts about climate, industries, natural wonders, resources, population, history, imports, and exports. For example, you may find in the atlas the location of Cairo, information on its climate, population statistics, and the names of local landmarks and monuments.

Some important atlases with which you should become acquainted are *National Geographic Atlas of the World, Rand McNally Popular World Atlas,* and *The Encyclopedia Britannica Atlas.*

ALMANACS

If your teacher asked you to name the source that would help your neighbor decide which phase of the moon would be appropriate for planting his short row of English peas, you would probably name the almanac. However, in what source would you find a list of all-star baseball games or a list of actors and actresses who won Academy Awards in 1984? Again, the answer is the almanac. Almanacs, which are published annually, are ideal sources for up-to-date, miscellaneous information on current events. The two most common almanacs that you will probably need to use are the *Information Please Almanac* and *The World Almanac and Book of Facts.* Remember, do not hesitate to ask the librarian for assistance when using the almanacs.

VERTICAL FILE

If you want to find a newspaper clipping on the poem that Maya Angelou read during President Clinton's inauguration, or if you want to read about Michael Jordan's retirement speech from basketball, then a perfect place to check is the library's vertical file. The vertical file is a storage or filing cabinet which contains pamphlets, newspaper clippings, and magazine clippings placed in a folder and then filed away in the cabinet for public use.

AUDIOS/VIDEOS

Have you thought about using cassette tapes, CDs, videos, and films as references in your research paper? There are many situations in which this is a good idea. If you are researching Shirley Temple or Michael Jordan, you may view some of her movies or his basketball games. If you are researching music of the 1960s, you may listen to music by the Beatles, the Doors, Elvis Presley, and Diana Ross and the Supremes.

21

OTHER RESOURCE MATERIALS

The library has many more reference materials with which you will become more familiar as you continue to work in the library. Your teacher will decide whether or not to introduce the following ones to you. Many of these references are also available on CD-ROMs.

African Art and Culture
    (videos and filmstrips)
African History on File
American Authors: 1600-1900
American Historical Images on File
    Collection: The Black Experience
American Men and Women of
    Science
American Women Writers
Bartlett's Familiar Quotations
Benet's Readers' Encyclopedia
Black Dramatists
British Authors of the Nineteenth
    Century
The Cambridge Encyclopedia
Chronicles of the 20th Century
The Civil Rights Movement
Contemporary Authors
Current Biography
Dictionary of American History
Dictionary of Cultural Literacy
Encyclopedia of Religion
Encyclopedia of the Social Sciences
Encyclopedia of Sports
European Authors 1000-1900
Harlem Renaissance and Beyond:
    Literary Biographies of 100
    Black Women Writers
Indians of North America (videos)
The International Cyclopedia of
    Music and Musicians
Masterpieces of World Literature
Microfiche

Microfilm
Minorities Have Made America
    Great (filmstrips)
More Super Trivia
Multicultural Peoples of North
    America (videos)
Oxford Companion to American
    Literature
Oxford Companion to English
    Literature
Oxford Companion to the Theatre
Oxford Dictionary of Quotations
The People's Almanac
Perspectives on Native Americans
    (videos)
Play Index
The Random House Children's
    Encyclopedia
Set on Freedom: The American Civil
    Rights Movement (multimedia)
Short Story Index
The Timetables of History
Today's Science on File
Today's Social Studies on File
Twentieth Century Authors
Values in America
    (videos—filmstrips)
Van Nostrand's Scientific
    Encyclopedia
A Woman's Place (video)
World Authors
World Biography
Yearbooks

Note: If your library does not have a certain book or article you need, your librarian should be able to special order the materials through the inter-library loan system.

Resource Materials

To answer the following questions, refer to an encyclopedia, dictionary, atlas, almanac, the *Readers' Guide to Periodical Literature*, vertical file, and any other resources necessary.

1. Who is the head librarian of your school? _____

2. Where would you look for an article on Michael Jordan's retirement speech from basketball? _____

3. What is the population of Atlanta, Georgia, the site for the 1996 World Olympics? _____

4. Name two novels written by E. B. White.
   a. _____
   b. _____

5. What source provides an explanation for the disappearance of dinosaurs? _____

6. List the birthdates and birthplaces of the following people:
   a. Mariah Carey _____ _____
   b. Bill Cosby _____ _____
   c. Stephen Spielberg _____ _____
   d. Bill Clinton _____ _____

7. Find a magazine article listed under one of the following subjects in the *Readers' Guide to Periodical Literature*. Copy the article's entry.
   a. Native Americans _____
   b. King Tutankhamen _____
   c. Disney World _____

8. List the word origin, part of speech, and definition for each of the following words.
   a. bicycle _____
   b. skate _____
   c. rap _____
   d. basketball _____

9. Answer the following about your home state.
   a. Capital city: _____
   b. Population: _____
   c. Biggest tourist attraction: _____
   d. Two state parks: _____
   _____

Name_____ Date _____

COMPUTERS AND THE LIBRARY

Because information is stored on computers in many libraries, books, periodicals, catalogs, and reference books have become increasingly more accessible to students. The computer can search for titles and locations of materials on any subject and display the information on the screen; you may also be able to print out a copy of the desired information.

A computer can also be useful for writing the research paper. You can make changes or edit your draft instantly and view the changes without retyping the entire paper. Also, depending on the type of software used, you may have access to "spellcheck" programs and other supplementary programs to help edit and proofread the final draft. If your library has computers that you do not know how to use properly, do not hesitate to ask the librarian for help.

AUTOMATED CARD CATALOG

In many schools the computerized (or automated) catalog has replaced the manual card catalog that typically stands somewhere in the middle of the library. With this computerized card catalog, the student can quickly acquire a printout of books on any given subject, as well as information on the availability of the books in the library.

CD-ROM (COMPACT DISC — READ-ONLY MEMORY)

Most encyclopedias now offer their information on CD-ROM (ROM, or Read-Only Memory, means that the user can access stored information but cannot change it). With an ever-expanding market availability, your school may have at least one CD-ROM file from *Compton's* or *Grolier's*. One CD-ROM can contain as much information as an entire set of encyclopedias. You can research pottery (ancient and contemporary), planets, volcanoes, dinosaurs, U.S. presidents, Mark Twain, and Beethoven's symphonies. The list is seemingly endless! CD-ROMs also combine text and pictures with sound. Not only can you find and read about Beethoven's Ninth Symphony but you can also hear it; you can see and hear John F. Kennedy and Martin Luther King, Jr., deliver some of their most famous speeches. You may also find CD-ROM files which contain articles in periodicals such as *Business Week, Newsweek, Ebony, Health, Discover,* and many others. The CD-ROM files have added new dimensions to research. With the addition of sounds and moving pictures, research has become more fun for everyone. Remember, you should be able to print out any text you need from a CD-ROM. Just ask your librarian for help!

ON-LINE NETWORK COMPUTER

The on-line network computer is becoming a popular reference tool in schools and libraries all over the world. This is a great telecommunications system which allows you to obtain information from places outside your school, even outside your own country. For example, if you are completing a unit in history on the Hawaiian Islands before they became part of the United States, you can use your computer to connect with particular schools in Hawaii and obtain the needed information. This type of system is key in bringing the world closer together. Students in Chicago, Illinois, will be able to call Hong Kong, London, Tokyo, or Paris when seeking information. Not only is text available, but sound and video images are also available to expand your awareness of the world. This telecommunications system allows you to interact daily with great amounts of data that are circling the globe at the speed of light. Exciting, isn't it?

VIRTUAL REALITY (VR)

Virtual reality is another computerized system which uses three-dimensional images, sound, and touch to form a setting that seems almost (virtually) real. In addition to appearing in arcades and shopping centers around the country, many schools (from primary grades through the university) are employing virtual reality in their libraries and classrooms. With this system, you can actually experience what you read in books, magazines, and other reading materials. To enter virtual reality, you must wear 3-D goggles that surround you with computer graphics. You can visit a virtually real museum, which includes the Mona Lisa, space photos, and a poster of Arnold Schwarzenegger as the Terminator. You can also meet Columbus or General Custer, or you can visit Mars. The unlimited experiences this computer system provides will allow you to play an even greater role in the research process.

COMPUTERS AND THE LIBRARY

Using the computers available in your library, answer the following questions.

1. Look up dinosaurs on your encyclopedia CD-Rom file and summarize an important fact from the entry.

   _____

   _____

2. Find out the types of references available in the computerized card catalog about the Bermuda (or Devil's) Triangle and list the names and call numbers of at least two books available in your library.

   a. _____

   b. _____

3. Using the *Readers' Guide to Periodical Literature* on computer (if possible), find two periodicals on Bo Jackson, and write their titles below.

   a. _____

   b. _____

4. Find a book or periodical on John F. Kennedy using the library's on-line computer.

   _____

5. Use your school's reference computer to locate a source on the music and American culture of the 1960s.

   _____

6. Use your school's reference computer to locate a source on Martin Luther King, Jr., and the Civil Rights Movement.

   _____

7. See if you can use the computer reference system to locate two sources on Native American tribes that occupied the Oklahoma territory.

   _____

   _____

*Name*_____   *Date* _____

Chapter Three

WRITING THE BIBLIOGRAPHY CARDS

If you plan to use information from a particular book, encyclopedia, magazine, or any other source, you must record and keep certain information to be used in your paper's bibliography. In addition to these more traditional resources, you may use television programs, lectures, interviews, letters, or surveys to provide references for your research paper. This reference information can be recorded on 3" x 5" index cards or sized slips of paper, thus allowing the cards to be easily placed in alphabetical order and making it easier for you to add or delete references without having to recopy your alphabetically-ordered list.

When you write your bibliography cards (or source cards), provide each card with a number which you may write in the upper right-hand corner of the card. As you begin taking notes, use the number of the bibliography card to help you identify each note card.

Depending on the type of resource you are using, you will need to write down different information on your bibliography card. If you use a book, you should record the following information:

1. Name of the author (last name first)
2. Title of the book (underlined)
3. Place of publication (city)
4. Name of the publisher
5. Year of publication (most recent year)

Your card should look like this:

⑤

Kuoche, Lawrence David. *The Bermuda Triangle Mystery - Solved*. New York: Harper & Row, 1975.

PLEASE NOTE: A comma is placed between the author's last and first names. A period is placed after the author's name and the book's title. *Be sure to underline the book's title.* Notice that a colon is placed after the city and a comma is inserted between the publisher and the year. Finally, a period is placed after the year.

If you use an encyclopedia, record the following information:

1. Name of the author of the article (if there is one)
2. Title of the article (in quotation marks)
3. Title of the encyclopedia (underlined)
4. Year of publication (edition)

> ②
>
> Burgess, Robert F. "The Bermuda Triangle." World Book Encyclopedia. 1978 ed.

PLEASE NOTE: If the article has an author, a comma is placed between the author's last and first names. A period is placed at the end of the article title and before the closing quotation marks. A period is also placed after the name of the encyclopedia. *Be sure to underline the name of the encyclopedia.* Notice that 'edition' is abbreviated as 'ed' (not capitalized) and is followed by a period.

> ③
>
> "Careers." Encyclopedia Americana. 1972 ed.

PLEASE NOTE: If the encyclopedia article does not have an author listed, begin the card with the article's title.

If you use a magazine or newspaper, record the following information:
1. Name of the author (if there is one)
2. Title of the article (in quotation marks)
3. Name of the magazine or newspaper (underlined)
4. Date of the magazine or newspaper
5. Page number(s) of the article

④

> Gordon, James Stewart. "What's the Truth About the Bermuda Triangle?" Reader's Digest. July, 1975: 75-79.

PLEASE NOTE: A comma is placed between the author's last and first names. A period is placed after the entire name. The article is placed within quotation marks, with a period inserted inside the closing quotation marks. The title of the magazine or newspaper is underlined. A comma is placed between the month and year. The date is followed by a colon. A period is placed after the page number(s). If the article begins on one page but is continued on a non-consecutive page, a comma is inserted between the page numbers (e.g., 33, 36, 44). If the article appears on consecutive pages, a hyphen is inserted between the page numbers (e.g., 33-36).

⑦

> "Olympics For Kids: Skaters on Cutting Edge of Style." The Atlanta Journal. Feb. 20, 1994: 6-2.

PLEASE NOTE: This example illustrates an unsigned article. The punctuation remains the same.

If you use a computer reference instead of the actual book, encyclopedia, or magazine to find information, you must still use the appropriate format to write your bibliography card. For example, if you reference the *Readers' Guide to Periodical Literature* on computer, then you should follow the format for writing a bibliography card for a magazine article. If you reference *Grolier's Encyclopedia* on computer, then you should follow the format for writing an encyclopedia bibliography card.

①

"Bo Jackson." *Grolier's Encyclopedia*. 1992 ed.

PLEASE NOTE: The above bibliography card is for an unsigned article found on the computer from *Grolier's Encyclopedia*.

If you use dictionaries, atlases, almanacs, vertical files, audio tapes, videotapes, television programs, movies, lectures, interviews, letters, surveys, or any other sources, you must make bibliography cards for them also, so ask your teacher for help recording the appropriate information in the correct form.

BIBLIOGRAPHY CARDS

Prepare bibliography cards using the following information. You may want to refer to pages 27-30 for help.

1. An unsigned article entitled Shirley Temple, Encyclopedia Americana, 1991.

2. A book entitled The Devil's Triangle, written by Elwood D. Baumann, published by Franklin Watts in New York, 1976.

3. A magazine article entitled Bo Jackson and Football, written by Steve Weff, in March 16, 1992, Sports Illustrated, page 80.

Name_____ Date _____

BIBLIOGRAPHY CARDS
A Cooperative Learning Activity

Work with three or four of your classmates to prepare each of the following bibliography cards.

1. A signed article entitled Falcon and Falconry in World Book Encyclopedia, written by Olin S. Pettingill, Sr. 1980.

2. A book entitled A Reader's Guide to Science Fiction, by Baird Searles and Martin Last, published by Facts on File, Inc., 1979, in New York.

3. A television program entitled The Jackson Family Honors on NBC, Feb. 22, 1994.

Name _____ Date _____

Chapter Four

TAKING NOTES

As you discover sources and begin to read about your research topic, you will also begin the process of taking notes. Taking notes is a very important part of the research paper process. One cannot expect to remember all that is read. Many writers decide to take notes on index cards or slips of paper, using a different card for each note. Some helpful hints for preparing your note cards are provided below.

1. Write in the top left-hand corner of the card a word or phrase that summarizes the information on the note card. Write on the front side of the note card only.

2. As you begin taking notes, write (in the top right-hand corner of the note card) the number from the bibliography card that lists the source of the information used.

3. Try to write the information on the note cards in your own words (in other words, paraphrase). Write only one idea per note card. Do not write notes from two sources on the same card.

4. If you must use quoted material, write the material enclosed in quotation marks. Limit your use of direct quotes when taking notes. You want to demonstrate that you are capable of expressing ideas in your own words.

5. At the bottom of every note card, write the page number from your source on which you find the information.

Writing Note Cards
With Direct Quotations

One of the easiest ways to take notes is to copy exactly the words of another person. Copying someone else's work in your paper and pretending that the work is yours is called plagiarism. If you do come across a line, sentence, or phrase that you want to copy into your paper, put quotation marks around the borrowed material and acknowledge where you got the information. However, a good research paper will not contain much copied material because a young research scholar will instead paraphrase ideas and then attempt to draw his or her own conclusions.

The following note card shows a direct quote. Note that the quoted material is placed within quotation marks.

```
Award                                    ②


  "The song 'On the Good Ship
   Lollipop' from the movie Bright
   Eyes won her an Academy Award."



              p. 458
```

Now It's Your Turn

Imagine that you are writing a research paper on dinosaurs. Your main idea is that dinosaurs resembled present-day birds more than present-day reptiles. Read the excerpt below and create a note card for it.

> For many years, people thought that dinosaurs were clumsy, slow-moving creatures that lived much like modern reptiles. However, fossil evidence shows that some kinds of dinosaurs—especially small theropods—probably were much more active than most present-day reptiles. In addition, most dinosaurs resembled birds, rather than modern reptiles, in their leg and foot structure and upright posture. Scientists generally agree that dinosaurs are closer ancestors of birds than of present-day reptiles. They believe that the study of birds can help us learn about the life of dinosaurs.

WRITING NOTE CARDS

Write note cards for each of the following selections.

Native Americans: Arts & Crafts
Middle American Indians created elaborate carvings. Large sculptures were used to decorate ancient Aztec and Maya structures or were placed alongside as monuments. Craftsmen also carved jade, onyx, quartz and other materials. The Northwest Coast Indians made fine wood carvings. Their ceremonial wooden masks had movable parts. They also carved house posts, grave markers, and totem poles.

Arts & Crafts: Carving
- -

The Indians usually combined painting with other arts. For example, much pottery of the Southwest Indians and of the Aztec, Maya and Inca had painted designs. The Aztec and Maya also made large wall paintings of important ceremonies and historic events. Painted designs also decorated some wood carvings of the northwest tribes. The Pueblo were the first to make sand paintings, and the Navajo improved on this ceremonial art.

Arts & Crafts: Painting
- -

Most Indian groups handed down their folk tales and poetry by word of mouth for centuries. Some North American Indians, such as the Chippewa, recorded some of their tribal songs on bark. The Maya left behind manuscripts that tell of their ancient history. The Inca wrote dramas dealing with great military victories as well as with everyday life.

Arts & Crafts: Literature
- -

Name _____   Date _____

EVALUATING NOTE CARDS
A Cooperative Learning Activity

Exchange the note cards for your research paper with those of a classmate and evaluate each other's cards. Then answer the following questions, keeping in mind how the note cards can be improved.

1. Do any of your partner's note cards appear to be unrelated to the main ideas? Explain.

   _____

   _____

   _____

2. Did you notice any cards without topic headings?

   _____

3. Do any cards have more than one idea per card? Are the ideas related or unrelated? Would you suggest making multiple cards from this card, or would you leave the card as your classmate has arranged it? Why?

   _____

   _____

   _____

4. Have you read any cards that have used direct quotations? Were the quotations correctly punctuated?

   _____

5. What did you discover to be most interesting about your classmate's notes? What was least interesting? Why?

   _____

   _____

   _____

6. After checking your partner's note cards, did you notice any misspelled words, incorrect punctuation, or omission of page numbers and source card numbers?

   _____

7. After reading your partner's note cards, what have you learned that would be helpful in writing your own cards?

   _____

   _____

_Name_____ _Date_ _____

Chapter Five

WRITING THE PRELIMINARY OUTLINE

Once you have chosen the topic for your research paper and have located and surveyed a number of resource materials, you are ready to list all of the points you wish to make or questions you wish to ask in the paper. When making this list, keep in mind a purpose statement or main idea (thesis) that you plan to focus on in your paper; this main idea can be included in the introductory paragraph. Your list of points will be organized into your outline.

The first (or preliminary) outline is intended to serve as a guide for writing your research paper. Begin the outline by thinking about your topic and asking yourself questions to discover the **major divisions** (main topics) and **subdivisions** (subtopics). Using the answers to your questions as your **headings** and **subheadings,** you may begin to write your preliminary outline. As you begin to read through your research, you will encounter some irrelevant (unimportant) points; of course, these can be eliminated. Your reading will also suggest new points that you will want to include in the paper; therefore, keep in mind that you can revise your preliminary outline as you take notes.

Follow these suggestions when writing your preliminary outline.

1. At the top of your outline page, write the title of your research paper.

2. Next, write the words "main idea" followed by your main idea statement. (This is your thesis statement.)

3. It is not necessary to include a great deal of detail in your first outline, but as you proceed you will naturally add more detail.

MAIN IDEA (THESIS STATEMENT)

The main idea (thesis) is one of the most important steps in developing your topic because it sets in motion your investigation of facts so that you can reach an original conclusion in your paper. You may think of the thesis statement as a road map, or a guide, to take you in the right direction. For example, if your subject is dinosaurs, and your topic is characteristics of carnivores, a possible thesis statement is: "Why are the Allosaurus and the Tyrannosaurus considered carnivorous dinosaurs?"

Here are three different thesis statements based on the same topic (the novel *Roll of Thunder, Hear My Cry*):

> **Roll of Thunder, Hear My Cry is a novel set in the back country of rural Louisiana along black and white racial boundaries during the post-depression era. The story is told by an adolescent black girl living in a household of three generations, including her two brothers, father, mother, and grandmother. This proud family, who had bought and maintained a large farm after Reconstruction, stands to lose its farm to a nearby greedy white farmer who has threatened them with scare tactics and white power.**

THESIS: _Roll of Thunder, Hear My Cry expresses the feelings of African American teenagers toward the violence against Blacks._

This student will examine African-American teenagers' feelings.

THESIS: _Roll of Thunder, Hear My Cry gives an outlook into the lives of young black Americans in a world of racial discrimination._

This student will look at racial discrimination against black Americans.

THESIS: _The issues that a young Black girl faces in her fight to be equal as whites is reflected in Roll of Thunder, Hear My Cry._

This student will explore the problems of a young black girl growing up in a segregated society.

Now It's Your Turn

In the space provided below, write a thesis statement (main idea) for *your* research paper.

_____

_____

_____

What Do You Think?

Now that you have written your thesis statement (main idea), check the box(es) below that apply to your purpose for writing this research paper.

- ❑ Is my thesis sentence a question? Do I offer an answer?
- ❑ Is my thesis a comparison of two or more things?
- ❑ Is my thesis a summary of information about my subject?
- ❑ Is my thesis proving or disproving a principle?

Cooperative Learning Activity

With a classmate, exchange and evaluate each other's thesis statement. After you have evaluated your classmate's thesis statement, ask yourself if you need to revise your own thesis statement.

Now that you have established your thesis statement, you should begin to think about writing your outline. Outlines can follow different sets of rules, and teachers' preferences may vary. Follow the outline form that your teacher wishes to use. A sample outline is listed below.

Title

I.	Main topic	(Introduction)
	A. Subtopic	(The background)
	B. Subtopic	(The problem)
	C. Subtopic	(The thesis statement)
II.	Main topic	(Body)
	A. Subtopic	(First major issue)
	B. Subtopic	(Second major issue)
	C. Subtopic	(Third major issue)
	1. Detail	(First minor issue)
	2. Detail	(Second minor issue)
III.	Main topic	(Conclusion)
	A. Subtopic	(Restate thesis statement)
	B. Subtopic	(Your final opinion)

In order to develop a preliminary outline, follow two easy steps: (1) write key words and phrases from your note cards and (2) separate your ideas into main topics and subtopics. Read the following passage written by Tonya Collins, a seventh grader:

> **The Bermuda Triangle has received much attention in the past few years. It has been the subject of many books, magazine articles, and radio and television talk shows. A television special was devoted to it, and it also figures in the UFO and ancient astronaut mysteries (Kusche 11). According to all accounts, there is something very strange going on out there.**

From the introductory paragraph above, notice the following key words that Tonya chose for her outline:

- magazine articles and books
- radio and television talk shows
- Bermuda Triangle
- UFO and mysteries

Tonya began by asking a few questions that helped in writing her paper.

1. Why has the Bermuda Triangle received so much attention?

2. What is the relationship between books, magazine articles, and radio and television talk shows?

3. What other accounts have been reported?

Like Tonya, you should first ask yourself what the main reason is for writing your research paper. As you think about this, make a list of issues which you plan to investigate.

After conducting research on her topic, Tonya decided to **examine** the following issues:
- the attention given to the Bermuda Triangle
- books that reveal that information
- magazine articles that reveal that information
- television talk shows
- UFOs and astronaut mysteries

Next, Tonya arranged her list of main topics and subtopics into a preliminary outline.

The Bermuda Triangle

Attention
    Books
    Magazine articles
    Radio and television talk shows
    UFOs and astronaut mysteries
Location
    440,000 square miles
    Florida, Bermuda, Puerto Rico
Mysteries
    Ships and aircrafts
    Mysterious winds
Explanations
    Outer space
    Disappearances
Conclusion
    Unknown
    Disturbances

Now It's Your Turn

For practice writing an outline, arrange the following list according to main topics and subtopics.

The World of Dinosaurs

reproduction	I. _____
land and climate	A. _____
growth	B. _____
food	II. _____
living habits	A. _____
kinds of dinosaurs	B. _____
environment of dinosaurs	III. _____
protection against enemies	A. _____
extinction of dinosaurs	B. _____
Saurischians	C. _____
Ornithischians	D. _____
plant and animal life	IV. _____

GUIDELINES FOR
WRITING AN OUTLINE

1. First, write the title of your paper across the top of the page.

2. Next, place a Roman numeral and a period before each main topic. Example: I. Rural life in Louisiana

3. When you divide the main topic into subtopics, be sure to place the A directly underneath the first letter of the first word of the main topic. Remember to place a period after the A and B (subtopics).
   Example: I. Later years of stardom
   >   A. Later movies
   >   B. Movie retirement

4. Please note in guideline #3 that if a main topic is divided, it must consist of at least two subtopics.

5. If you are using words or phrases, not sentences, in your outline, do not place a period after a main topic or a subtopic. Example: II. Kinds of dinosaurs

6. Begin the main topic and subtopic with a capital letter, and capitalize any proper nouns.

7. An outline should use parallel structure—the use of the same kind of word or phrase. Incorrect: I. Later years of stardom
   >   A. Later movies
   >   B. When did she retire from movies?

This example is incorrect because the topic and first subtopic are written as phrases and the second subtopic is written as a complete sentence (a question). The structure is not parallel.

The following is a sample outline on "The Life and Times of Bo Jackson" by Keith Cooley, a sixth grader.

The Life and Times of Bo Jackson

I. Early Life
A. Family
B. School
II. College Years
A. Football
B. Track
C. Baseball
III. Professional Sports Career
A. Football
B. Baseball
C. Short Comeback
IV. Adult Life
A. Family
B. Sports endorsements

Now It's Your Turn

Fill in the blanks of this incomplete outline with the most appropriate items listed at the right.

The Lifetime Career of Shirley Temple*

I.   Early years

     A. _____   national positions

     B. _____   later movies

     C. Movies with "Bojangles" Robinson   early childhood

                                            movie retirement

II.   Later years of stardom   first movies

     A. _____   after movies

     B. _____

III.   A. Marriage

     B. _____

Preliminary outline of Heather Rushing, an eighth grade student

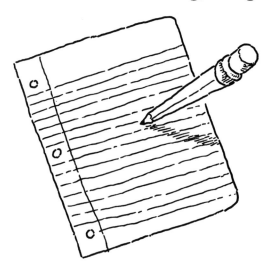

Name _____   Date _____

WRITING THE PRELIMINARY OUTLINE

On a separate sheet of paper, make a list of topics related to your subject. You may add to this list any other points of interest that you have discovered in your reading. Organize this information into main topics, subtopics, and details. In the space provided below, write your preliminary outline. Remember that this is not your final outline.

Name_____   Date _____

43

EVALUATING THE PRELIMINARY OUTLINE
A Cooperative Learning Activity

Exchange your preliminary outline with a classmate. Evaluate your classmate's outline by answering the following questions. (Keep in mind that your outline will be improved by someone else's suggestions.)

1. First, read the entire preliminary outline. Did the outline begin with the title of the paper? Yes___ No___ If yes, after reading the outline, do you think the title is appropriate? Yes___ No___ If no, what do you think the title should be?

   _____

2. What heading(s) or subheading(s) should be omitted, changed, or added to the outline?

   _____

3. Has your classmate used correct outline form to indicate subtopic(s)? Yes___ No___ If not, which subtopic(s) would you rewrite?

   _____

   _____

4. Is any subtopic placed under the wrong main topic? Yes___ No___ If yes, name the subtopic and tell where you would place it.

   _____

   _____

5. Are all the topics and subtopics lined directly under one another so that all capital letters and numerals are aligned properly? Yes___ No___ If not, where would you make changes?

   _____

   _____

6. What is your overall impression of your classmate's outline?

   _____

   _____

7. Can you suggest any further improvements?

   _____

   _____

Name_____ Date _____

Chapter Six

DOCUMENTING YOUR SOURCES

Parenthetical Documentation

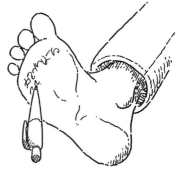

In the past, endnotes and footnotes have been used to recognize the sources and authors used in the research paper. Endnotes are placed at the end of the paper on a separate page. Footnotes are written at the bottom (foot) of each page. Recently, the most common practice in most middle and high schools and colleges is to use parenthetical documentation (or in-text citation). Documentation means that you have made a reference to your source and you are giving credit to that source. In parenthetical documentation, you state the author's last name and the page number on which you found your information within parentheses following the sentence that contains the cited information. For example, (Burgess 208).

Guidelines For Documenting Sources (Giving Credit)

1. If you "borrow" (copy) information directly from a source, then you must place the information within quotation marks. Follow the quote with the author's last name and the page number on which you found the information within parentheses and followed by a period.
   "If a man does not keep pace with his companions . . . perhaps he steps to the beat of a different drummer" (Thoreau 124).

2. If you write information in your own words (paraphrase), and the information contains important ideas and facts you did not know, **do not** place the information in quotation marks. The information should be followed by the author's last name and page number within parentheses and followed by a period.
   Since 1954, more than 50 ships and aircraft have vanished in or near the Bermuda Triangle (Burgess 208).

3. Notice that in the following example there is no punctuation (comma) between the author and page number. Do not use the words "page," "pages," or the abbreviations "p." or "pp." Example: **(Burgess 208).**

4. If you use the author's name in a paraphrase or quotation, then do not place the author's name in parentheses at the end of the sentence.
   Burgess stated that since 1954 more than 50 ships and aircraft have vanished in or near the Bermuda Triangle (208).

5. When there is no stated author, place the name of the source and page number within parentheses.
   When she was young, she was a political activist for the Republican Party (<u>Academic American Encyclopedia</u> 99).

6. When there are two authors for one work, state both last names separated by "and." For example, **(Graham and Ledbetter 46).** If there are three authors, give each last name of the authors with the final name preceded by "and." For example, **(Witting, Barry, and Harvey 125).** *Note: Commas follow Witting and Barry.*

7. If there are more than three authors for one source, use the first author's last name, followed by **"et al."** (Latin for "and others"). For example, **(Brandes et al. 32).**

8. If your sources have two or more authors with the same last names, write both the first and last names of the authors in the parentheses to distinguish between or among them. For example, **(Robert Burgess 208).**

9. If you are citing two or more works by the same author(s), put a comma after the last name(s) of the author(s) followed by the title of the work and the page reference. For example, **(Burgess, "The Bermuda Triangle" 208).**

10. When you are citing the title of a magazine article with no author given, it is permissible to shorten the title to a key word (or words) for the documentation. Remember, though, you must give the full title on the bibliography page. For example, if the title of the article is **"Artificial Hip Goes Pro With Bo,"** your citation may read **("Artificial Hip" 10).**

   Note: You do not need to document information that is considered common knowledge.

Now It's Your Turn

1. Write the parenthetical documentation for the article "The Bermuda Triangle" by Robert Burgess from page 208 of <u>World Book Encyclopedia</u>. The following is an excerpt from Tonya Collins' research paper.
   The first recorded disappearance of a U.S. ship in the Bermuda Triangle occurred in March, 1918, when the <u>U.S.S. Cyclops</u> vanished. On December 5, 1945, a squadron of five U.S. bombers disappeared, and a seaplane vanished while looking for the aircraft (   ).

2. Read the following passage written by Keith Cooley. He has paraphrased information taken from the article "Artificial Hip Goes Pro With Bo" with no author from <u>Sports Illustrated</u>. (Observe how he has included a direct quotation within quotation marks.) Write the parenthetical documentation for Keith's passage from page 10.
   After his hip replacement, Bo trained for almost a year to strengthen his leg and hip. In 1993, he returned to professional baseball with the Chicago White Sox. In his first time at bat in the regular season, he hit a home run. <u>Sports Illustrated</u> called it "the greatest comeback of them all" (   ).

Footnotes

Even though most English teachers require students to follow the MLA (Modern Language Association) guide in writing their research papers (which asks students to document sources using parenthetical documentation), some teachers still require the use of footnotes. As stated earlier, a footnote is a numbered reference placed at the bottom (foot) of the page. To decide if a source should be footnoted in your paper, use the following guidelines:

1. When you are copying the exact words from a source, always enclose the entire quote in quotation marks.

2. When you are paraphrasing (rephrasing) someone else's idea that is an opinion and is not common knowledge, use a footnote. It is not necessary to use a footnote when paraphrasing facts that are considered common knowledge.

3. Use a footnote when statements are used that appear to be contrary to popular belief.

4. Use a footnote to document unusual or rare facts or statistics that may appear in only one source.

5. To properly indicate a footnote in your paper, write a number slightly above and to the right of the punctuation mark at the end of a sentence, clause, or phrase that includes a quotation or an idea from a source. Begin with number "1" and continue numbering the footnotes consecutively throughout the paper.

6. To avoid having to rewrite or retype a page, plan ahead to have enough space for all of the footnotes. For example, if you have indicated in your text that you have quoted two sources, then at the bottom of that page you must correctly number and indicate two footnotes.

When writing the footnotes, be sure to include all of the necessary information in correct order. Note in the example below the correct items and order for the first time use of a source. Footnotes are ordered and punctuated similarly to sources in the bibliography. Remember that each footnote ends with a period.

1. Footnote for an encyclopedia article:

    [1]"Shirley Temple," <u>Encyclopedia Americana</u>, 1991, Vol. 23, 576.
    (If the article has an author, the author's name is placed first—first name followed by last name.)

2. Footnote for a book:

    [1]Lawrence David Kusche, <u>The Bermuda Triangle Mystery—Solved</u> (New York: Harper and Row, 1975) 11.

3. Footnote for a magazine article:

    [2]Steve Wuff, "Bo Jackson and Football," <u>Sports Illustrated</u> (March 16, 1992): 80.

TO DOCUMENT OR NOT TO DOCUMENT

Read each of the following statements. If you think the statement requires documentation, check **yes** and then give a reason why you would use parenthetical documentation or footnotes. If **no**, explain why not.

1. The song "On the Good Ship Lollipop" from the movie *Bright Eyes* won her an academy award.
   Yes___ No___ _____

   _____

2. Scientists generally agree that dinosaurs are closer ancestors of birds than of present-day reptiles.
   Yes___ No___ _____

   _____

3. Martin Luther King, Jr., was a famous African-American civil rights leader during the 1960s.
   Yes___ No___ _____

   _____

4. Some North American Indians, such as the Chippewa, recorded some of their tribal songs on bark.
   Yes___ No___ _____

   _____

5. Nancy Kerrigan won a silver medal and Tonya Harding placed eighth in the ice skating competition of the 1994 Winter Olympics.
   Yes___ No___ _____

   _____

6. The Mexican culture is a prime example of Mestizo, which was derived from an advanced Indian culture and the Spanish culture.
   Yes___ No___ _____

   _____

*Name*_____ *Date* _____

Chapter Seven

WRITING THE FIRST DRAFT

Using your note cards and preliminary outline as references, you are now ready to write the first draft of your research paper. As you write the first draft, concentrate only on putting your ideas on paper. Do not worry about spelling, grammar, or punctuation. Schedule your time wisely so that you will have time to reexamine your work to determine what needs to be revised or deleted. The following evaluation guidelines will help you in writing the first draft.

Introduction:	• The introduction may be one or two paragraphs.
	• Your thesis statement (main idea) is often effective when written as the last sentence in the introductory paragraph.
	• Keep in mind that the purpose of the introduction is to grab the reader's attention.
Body:	• Your next step is to separate your note cards according to the main topics and subtopics as shown on your outline.
	• Begin to read your note cards aloud. If you discover you have two or more cards with similar information, place them together.
	• Read the cards again for logical order. Turn the note cards over as you use them in your draft. Do not discard any cards, as you may be able to use them later.
Documentation:	• Make sure your sources are properly documented in the paper. You should use the MLA format of parenthetical documentation or another acceptable format (either footnotes or endnotes). If you use a word-for-word quotation, be sure to enclose it in quotation marks and identify the source.
Conclusion:	• The conclusion, signaling that the paper is coming to an end, may be one or two paragraphs and should summarize the main ideas given in the paper. The conclusion may be based on your opinion and need not contain any new information or documentation.

EDITING THE FIRST DRAFT

Practice editing the following paragraph (first draft) written by a seventh grader. In rewriting the paragraph, feel free to change any of the words, place the sentences in a more logical order, and remove any sentences that do not agree with the main topic. Also, correct any errors in spelling, capitalization, and punctuation.

Heart Attacks: Cause, Prevention, and Treatment

a heart attack refers to when a blood clot blocks the flow of one or more of your coronary artaries. When the blood flow is cut of the cells do not recieve the oxygen that they need this causes the blood supply to an area of the muscle to be cut off causing this portion of the muscle to dye (Mayo Clinic 45). Men in their forties are more likely to have a heart attach than women. The seriousness of this depends on where the blockage occurs ("Heart Attack" 62).

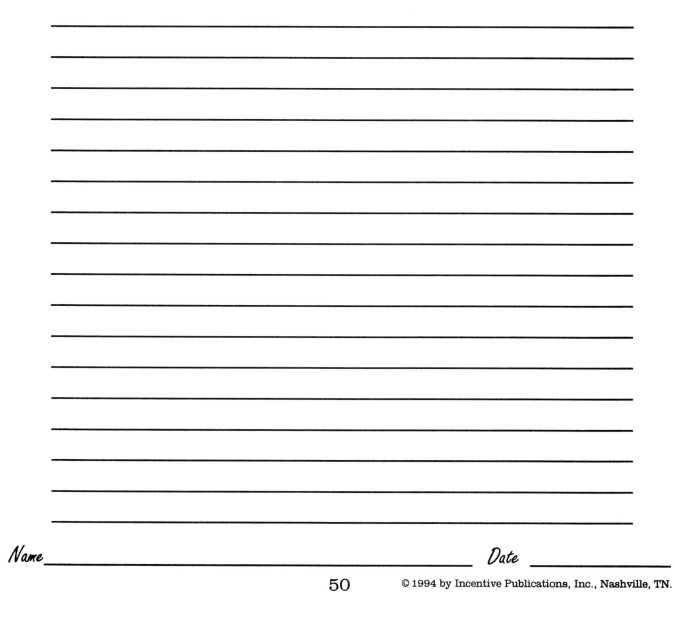

Name_____ Date _____

Sample First Draft

Notice that student Frank Loftis' outline and first draft (shown here on pages 51-53) support and develop his thesis statement. As you read Frank's outline and draft, notice that he has organized his paragraphs based on the points and details taken from his note cards. Remember, as you write your first draft, review your notes and note cards and organize them carefully.

OUTLINE

Thesis: Shakespeare was a man of many qualities & talents, & he proved so when he got to London by the building of his renowned Globe Theater.

I. William Shakespeare
   A. Early Life
   B. Family
   C. Education
   D. Achievements

II. Globe Theater
   A. Plays
   B. Actors
   C. Audience
   D. Levels

III. Globe Theater
   A. Fire
   B. Rebuilding

Change sentence structure to be more concise and less wordy.

Notice the location of the thesis statement.

Transition shifts to the body of the paper.

Source has been properly documented (however, no comma is needed).

Addition of a word for clarity

Spelling error

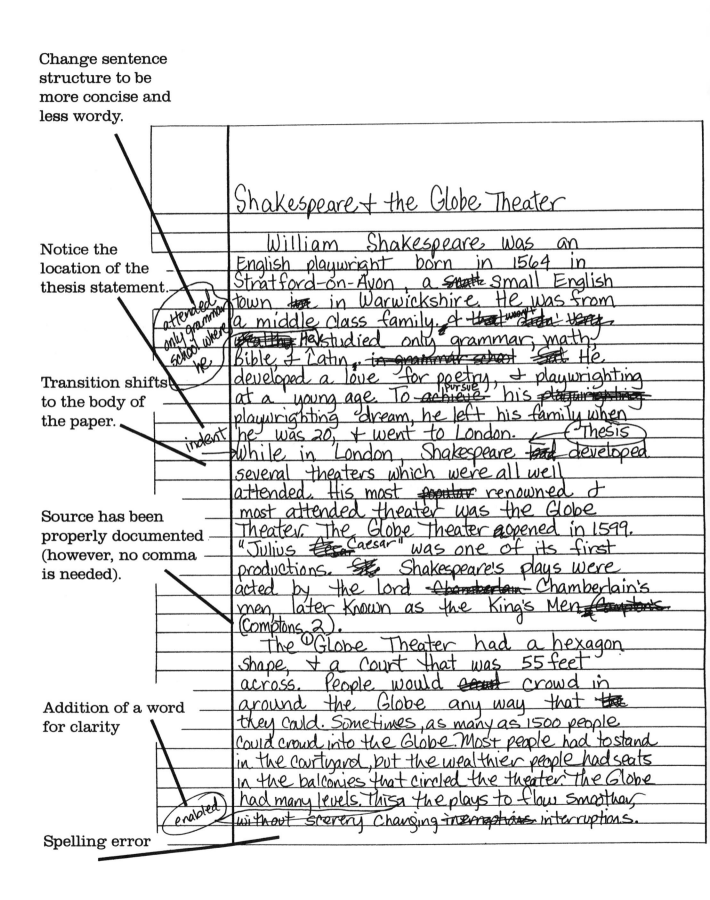

Shakespeare + the Globe Theater

William Shakespeare, was an English playwright born in 1564 in Stratford-on-Avon, a small English town in Warwickshire. He was from a middle class family. He studied only grammar, math, bible, + Latin. He developed a love for poetry, + playwrighting at a young age. To pursue his playwrighting dream, he left his family when he was 20, + went to London. — Thesis

While in London, Shakespeare developed several theaters which were all well attended. His most renowned + most attended theater was the Globe Theater. The Globe Theater opened in 1599. "Julius Caesar" was one of its first productions. Shakespeare's plays were acted by the lord Chamberlain's men, later known as the King's Men (Comptons 2).

The Globe Theater had a hexagon shape, + a court that was 55 feet across. People would crowd in around the Globe any way that they could. Sometimes, as many as 1500 people could crowd into the Globe. Most people had to stand in the courtyard, but the wealthier people had seats in the balconies that circled the theater. The Globe had many levels. This the plays to flow smoother, without scenery changing interruptions.

Delete
unnecessary
words.

Incorrect
documentation
of a computer
source

Incorrect
punctuation

Avoid
abbreviations
and word
symbols.

Restate subject
for clarity
(clearness).

Does the
concluding
paragraph
restate the
thesis?

Capitalize all
proper names.

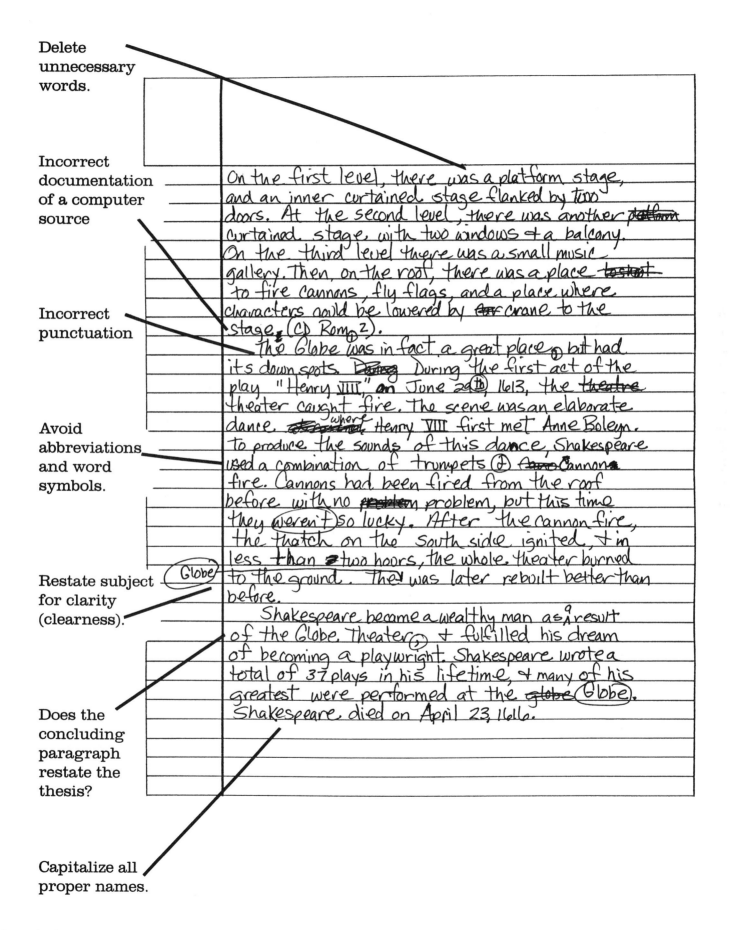

On the first level, there was a platform stage,
and an inner curtained stage flanked by two
doors. At the second level, there was another ~~platform~~
curtained stage, with two windows & a balcony.
On the third level there was a small music
gallery. Then, on the roof, there was a place ~~to shoot~~
to fire cannons, fly flags, and a place where
characters could be lowered by ~~for~~ crane to the
stage. (CD Rom 2).
        The Globe was in fact a great place but had
it's down spots. ~~During~~ During the first act of the
play "Henry VIII," ~~on~~ June 29th, 1613, the ~~theatre~~
theater caught fire. The scene was an elaborate
dance. ~~where~~ Henry VIII first met Anne Boleyn.
To produce the sounds of this dance, Shakespeare
used a combination of trumpets & ~~cannon~~ Cannon
fire. Cannons had been fired from the roof
before with no ~~problem~~ problem, but this time
they weren't so lucky. After the cannon fire,
the thatch on the south side ignited, & in
less than two hours, the whole theater burned
(Globe) to the ground. They was later rebuilt better than
before.
        Shakespeare became a wealthy man as a result
of the Globe Theater & fulfilled his dream
of becoming a playwright. Shakespeare wrote a
total of 37 plays in his lifetime, & many of his
greatest were performed at the ~~globe~~ (Globe).
Shakespeare died on April 23, 1616.

WRITING THE FIRST DRAFT

In the space provided below, write your introductory paragraph(s), including the thesis statement. Then continue writing your first draft on notebook paper, inserting the proper parenthetical documentation (if your teacher is instructing you to use the MLA format).

Name_____ Date _____

EVALUATING THE FIRST DRAFT
A Cooperative Learning Activity

Working with your classmates, read and discuss each other's drafts. Respond to the following questions as you read a classmate's draft. Then use your classmate's comments to help you revise your own draft.

1. First, read the introduction. Can you pick out your classmate's topic and thesis statement? On the lines below, write your classmate's thesis.

   _____

   _____

   _____

2. Is your classmate's thesis clear? Too limited? Too broad? Do you have any suggestions for rewriting it?

   _____

   _____

   _____

3. Is the introduction interesting? Did it immediately "grab your attention"? If not, suggest ways to improve the introduction.

   _____

   _____

   _____

4. Next, read the body of the draft. Write the main ideas and then locate the supporting details that accompany each idea. Point out to your classmate any main ideas that lack clear, supporting ideas.

   _____

   _____

   _____

Name_____ Date _____

5. After reading the draft, what do you feel is its most fascinating aspect? Why is it fascinating? What is its least fascinating aspect? Suggest ways for improvement.

    _____

    _____

    _____

6. Are there any sentences misplaced (out of logical order)? If so, suggest a more logical order. Do the sentences flow in a rhythmic transition within the paragraphs? If not, suggest ways for improvement.

    _____

    _____

    _____

7. Has your classmate supplied enough background information? If not, what do you suggest?

    _____

    _____

    _____

8. Has your classmate documented the sources in the first draft? If not, can you detect what has been "copied" or paraphrased and what actually belongs to your classmate? If the information has been copied, is it enclosed within quotation marks?

    _____

    _____

    _____

9. Read the conclusion. Is the thesis restated? Do the main topics support the thesis statement in a concluding statement?

    _____

    _____

    _____

*Name*_____ *Date* _____

Chapter Eight

WRITING THE FINAL OUTLINE

If, after carefully reviewing your note cards and preliminary outline, you realize that no further research is necessary, it is time to write your final outline. Read each line of your preliminary outline and your note cards to determine if there are any topics or subtopics that lack enough supporting information. On the lines provided, indicate any of these topics or subtopics that require more research.

_____

_____

_____

_____

Guidelines For Writing The Final Outline

Remember, if your final outline is well organized, your whole paper will probably be organized, too.

1. In writing your final outline, keep in mind that you can write either a topic outline or a sentence outline. (A topic outline uses words or phrases; a sentence outline is written in complete sentences.)

2. A thesis statement (main idea of the paper) is included in the introductory paragraph(s). Often it is the last sentence.

3. The introductory paragraph (the first main topic of your outline) states the main objective for writing the research paper.

4. The body of the paper reflects the main topics and subtopics on your outline. The body presents information which supports your thesis and is presented in paragraph form.

5. A conclusion (the last main topic on the outline) summarizes the main points examined in the body of the paper.

Review student Heather Rushing's final outline. Pay attention to how she organized and incorporated the guidelines for revising her final outline.

Title of the paper

Capitalize the first word of each main topic and subtopic.

If there is an A, there must be a B; if there is a 1, there must be a 2.

Notice how the subtopics (A, B, C) fall directly under the D in "During."

Parallel structure (same kind of word or phrase) is used in the main topics (I, II, III). All are prepositional phrases.

The Life of Shirley Temple

I. During the early years
   A. Early childhood
   B. First movies
   C. Movies with "Bojangles"

II. In later years of stardom
   A. Later movies
   B. Movie retirement

III. After movies
   A. Marriage
   B. National positions

This outline, written by student Tonya Collins, follows the guidelines for writing a final outline.

The Bermuda Triangle

I. Introduction
   A. Media events
   B. No calls for help
   C. "All is well."

II. Location
   A. 440,000 square miles
   B. Florida, Bermuda, Puerto Rico

III. Legend
   A. Military crafts
   B. Christmas Winds
   C. U.S.S. Cyclops

IV. Opinions
   A. Flying saucer
   B. Disintegration

V. Conclusion
   A. Natural force
   B. Atmospheric disturbance
   C. Gravitational disturbance
   D. Electromagnetic disturbance

Now It's Your Turn

Answer the following questions based on the above outline.

1. What are the five main topics? a. _____

                         b. _____

                         c. _____

                         d. _____

                         e. _____

2. List two subtopics under the topic **Legend.** 1. _____

                                       2. _____

3. Has Tonya used parallel structure in her outline? Yes ____ No ____

Name_____ Date _____

Student Frank Loftis' final outline provides another example of correct organization, style, punctuation, capitalization, and parallel structure.

Shakespeare and the Globe Theater

I. William Shakespeare
  A. Early life
  B. Family
  C. Education
  D. Achievements

II. Globe Theater
  A. Plays
  B. Actors
  C. Audience
  D. Levels

III. Globe Theater Fire
  A. Burning
  B. Rebuilding

IV. Conclusion

Now It's Your Turn

On a separate sheet of paper, rewrite this outline using a different (but still parallel) structure.

WRITE YOUR FINAL OUTLINE

After reviewing your preliminary outline(s) and notes, as well as the sample final outlines on pages 58-60, write your final outline on the lines provided below.

Name_____   Date _____

EVALUATING THE FINAL OUTLINE
A Cooperative Learning Activity

Working with a classmate, read and discuss each other's final outline. Answer the following questions as you read your classmate's outline. Then you may use your classmate's comments to help you in revising your final outline.

1. First, read the outline carefully. Is the outline written in topic or sentence form? Topic _____ Sentence _____ If not properly written in either topic or sentence form, what changes should be made?

   _____

   _____

   _____

2. After reading the outline, do you detect any errors in spelling, punctuation, or capitalization? Yes _____ No _____ If yes, state the errors.

   _____

   _____

   _____

3. Does the outline reflect an introduction, body, and conclusion? Yes _____ No _____ If no, which section(s) needs improving?

   _____

   _____

   _____

4. Are the main topics and subtopics lined directly under one another so that all capital letters and numerals are aligned? Yes _____ No _____ If no, where would you make changes?

   _____

   _____

5. Is the outline written in parallel structure (using the same kind of wording or phrasing)? For example, are the main topics written in prepositional phrases? in verb phrases? in nouns? in complete sentences? If not, **suggest** ways to revise so that the outline is parallel.

   _____

   _____

   _____

Name _____ *Date* _____

Chapter Nine

REVISING AND REWRITING THE FIRST DRAFT

Revising and rewriting the research paper are the final stages of the writing process. This is the time for you to make any changes to improve the ideas expressed in your paper. (Keep in mind that even the best writers hardly ever create a masterpiece in writing their first draft!) As you begin to revise and rewrite your first draft, think of ways you can improve your selection of words, transitions, and parallel structure (in sentences and paragraphs). Review the following guidelines before revising and rewriting your first draft.

Guidelines For Revising And Rewriting The First Draft

1. **"Let it rest for awhile."** Give yourself time to write the first draft and then put it aside for a few days. During this time, you can reflect on what you have written. Students often find that after a few days, their thoughts become more organized.

2. **Grab the reader's attention.** Make sure that your introductory paragraph catches the reader's attention and introduces the thesis statement.

3. **Reread your draft aloud.** Are there any sentences or paragraphs that sound out of place or are poorly written? If so, indicate these in the margins of your paper.

4. **Develop and use a system for making corrections.** Mark through words, phrases, and sentences that need revising. Do not eliminate anything yet as you may be able to use the information later.

5. **Make your thesis easy to follow.** Each paragraph should contain a topic sentence with supporting details. Each supporting sentence in each paragraph should relate to the topic sentence.

6. **Check to make sure your sentences are clearly written and easy to read.** Add transitional words (**e.g., while, after, since, although, first, next, further, also, finally, furthermore, in addition, consequently**) to show how ideas are related to one another.

7. **Check your paper for accuracy.** Check punctuation, spelling, word usage, and capitalization. Consider asking a classmate, friend, parent, relative, or another teacher to assist in checking for accuracy.

8. **Be sure that your sources are properly documented.** If sections of the paper are not written in your own words, make sure that you have given proper credit for "borrowing" the writer's words (either quoted directly or paraphrased). Place quotation marks around another writer's exact words.

9. **Add a title page and outline.** Make sure you have correctly written a title page and outline according to your teacher's specifications.

10. **Proofread your research paper carefully.** Your final copy should be error-free and neat.

11. **Restate your thesis in the concluding paragraph.** Reword your main idea for the final (restated) thesis in the concluding paragraph.

12. **Write the final copy in ink, or type it using a typewriter or a personal computer.** Write or type on only one side of the paper. Number the pages in the upper right-hand corner of each page, beginning with the second page. Double-space the paper if you are typing it.

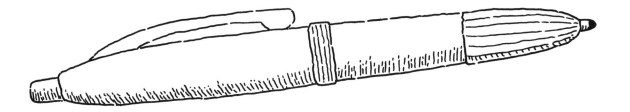

Student Samples

Review some of the student samples on the following pages to help you in revising your research paper. As you study the models, consider why the revisions were needed.

The Bermuda Triangle

The Bermuda Triangle, which has received much attention in the past few years; It has been the subject of many books, magazine articles, and radio and television talk shows. A television special was devoted to it, and it also, the Bermuda Triangle figures in the U.F.O. and ancient astronaut mysteries. According to all accounts, there is something very strange occurring going on out there (Kusche, Lawrence David, p. 11).

In this particularly stormy and changeable patch of ocean called the Bermuda Triangle, ship and plane losses can be sudden, surprising and total. Frequently, there are no calls for help, no survivors, no bodies, and no wreckage. A ship may sail into a calm sea under a cloudless sky — then vanish. A plane may disappear there, after reporting that "all is well." I believe that some people that have supposedly disappeared in the Triangle have been captured by countries such as Cuba (Cusack 68).

- Use a clause to combine sentences.
- Two separate ideas are stated but need proper transition.
- Word choice is improved.
- Only last name of author is necessary.
- Transition is correctly used.
- Check for misspelled words.
- Avoid using "I believe" and "I think."
- Improper documentation

Student Samples, continued

Numbers whose names consist of more than two words should be written as numerals.

No comma or page abbreviation is needed for documentation.

These ideas and facts are related and should be included in one paragraph.

Note the clarity and transition between sentences.

Check for misspelled words.

Underline the names of ships and planes.

Note the coordination of two thoughts and proper use of the comma.

Commercial and military craft cross this area safely every day. Since 1954, more than 50 ships and aircrafts have vanished in or near the Bermuda Triangle (Burgess, 208).

Of the alleged ships and planes lost mysteriously during the last 100 years, most have met misfortune in the months of December and January. During these months, Boreal blasts and the Christmas winds blow across the Triangle, bringing huge swells. Three of the most celebrated victims have disappeared on the same date: December 5 (Gordon, 75-79).

The first recorded disappearance of a U.S. ship in the Bermuda Triangle occurred in March, 1918, when the U.S.S. Cyclops vanished. On December 5, 1945, a squadron of 5 U.S. bombers disappeared, and a sea-plane vanished while looking for the aircraft (Burgess, 208).

Student Samples, continued

Read and observe the following sixth grader's first attempt at organizing and writing this research paper, using his personal computer.

Bo Jackson

No thesis sentence in the introductory paragraph

Bo Jackson was born on November 30, 1962 in Bessemer, Alabama, just south of Birmingham. He was the eighth of ten children and grew up in a family without much money.

Lack of paragraph organization and structure. Combine third paragraph with first; combine fourth paragraph with second.

Bo explained his tough childhood in his book <u>Bo Knows Bo</u> (1990): "We never had enough food. But at least I could beat on the other kids and steal their lunch money and buy myself something to eat. But I couldn't steal a father."

His family remembers him as a rowdy child and so they called him "boarhog." The nickname by which the whole world knows him is an abbreviation of the expression "bo hog."

Vague, unclear word choice and sentence structure

As a child, Bo developed a deep love for his family, in particular his mother, and a profound spirituality. When he was thirteen, he even planned to become a Baptist preacher.

No comma or page abbreviation is needed in documentation.

Bo played Little League baseball for only two weeks because his coaches thought he was ~~to~~ _top_ rough. They pushed him to the Pony League, and ~~it~~ ~~was~~ not long be~~fore~~ _after_ he was playing in a semi-pro men's league (<u>Bo Jackson</u> ~~ps~~. 38).

Good choice of transition and parallel verb structure

By the time he was a ninth grader at McAdory High School, Bo played both sports, and college recruiters began to take notice. <u>Bo</u> was first recognized nationally in 1982 when the N.Y. Yankees offered him a multi-year contract. <u>Bo</u> was still a senior in high school at the time. He thought a long time about accepting the Yankees' offer but turned it down to attend Auburn University in Auburn, Alabama.

Avoid beginning every sentence with a subject.

Note the use of the possessive case.

Student Samples, continued

Number each
page after the
first.

Combine
sentences into
one paragraph.

This statement
supports the
main idea with
interesting
facts and
statistics.

Capitalize
proper nouns.

Begin new
paragraph—
shift in
thought.

Underline or
italicize titles of
magazines.

In documentation,
titles of magazine
articles are placed
within quotation
marks.

Bo broke all of Auburn's football rushing records, becoming the first Auburn back ever to rush in excess of 4,000 yards in a career (Eiland   1168).

As a freshman and as a sophomore, Bo lettered in track. In 1985, starting as center fielder for the baseball team, he batted .401 with 17 home runs and 43 runs batted in.

He capped off his collegiate career by winning the fifty-first annual Heisman Trophy as the outstanding college football player in America.

Bo surprised football fans by choosing a baseball career with Kansas City, but in 1986 the L.A. Raiders asked him to reconsider football. In 1987, he signed a five year contract worth $7.4 million. He excelled in both sports, but in early March, 1991, his career as a two-sport pro athlete was somewhat derailed. On January 13, he had partially dislocated his left hip during a football game, severing the blood vessels that nourish the bones of the hip socket. On April 4, 1992, Jackson's injured hip was replaced with an artificial one. After his hip replacement Bo trained for almost a year to strengthen his leg and hip. In 1993 he returned to professional baseball with the Chicago White Sox. In his first time at bat in the regular season, he hit a home run. Sports Illustrated called it "the greatest comeback of them all" (Artificial Hip 10).

The six feet one inch and two-hundred and twenty-five pound athlete is married and has three children. His wife,

Now It's Your Turn

Referring to the "Guidelines for Revising and Rewriting the First Draft" on pages 63-64 and excerpts of the students' research papers on pages 65-68, read and revise your own first draft.

Preparing Your First Bibliography

A bibliography is a list of the sources (books, encyclopedia articles, magazine articles, pamphlets, newspaper articles, films, interviews, lectures, letters, and television programs) that you have used to write your research paper. The bibliography is to be placed on the last page of your research paper. Because you have already made a bibliography card for each of your sources, all you need to do to prepare your bibliography is to alphabetize the cards by authors' last names. If the source does not include an author, alphabetize the bibliography card according to the first word in the title.

Read the sample bibliography below. Note how the second line (as well as the third line) of each entry is indented.

BIBLIOGRAPHY

Bibliography

Baumann, Elwood D. *The Devil's Triangle*. New York: Franklin Watts, 1976. — (Book)

Burgess, Robert F. "The Bermuda Triangle." *World Book Encyclopedia*. 1978. — (Encyclopedia Article)

Cusack, Michael J. *Is There a Bermuda Triangle?* New York: Messner, 1976. — (Book)

Gordon, James S. "What's the Truth About the Bermuda Triangle?" *Reader's Digest*. July, 1975: 75-79. — (Magazine Article)

Kusche, Lawrence D. *The Bermuda Triangle Mystery—Solved*. New York: Harper & Row, 1975. — (Book)

WRITING YOUR FIRST BIBLIOGRAPHY

In the space provided below, use the information from your bibliography cards to construct your first bibliography. Write it in the space provided below. Do not forget to alphabetize your list according to the authors' last names.

Name_____   Date _____

Chapter Ten

WRITING OR TYPING THE FINAL PAPER

You are now in the final stages of writing your research paper. What do you do next? Before you begin hand-writing or typing your paper, keep in mind that your final paper should be neat as well as complete. Proofreading in this near-final stage is crucial because you are able to check your final draft one last time for organization, clarity, parallel structure, spelling, punctuation, and word choice. You may find that using a computer to write your research paper saves time. The computer allows you to store and retrieve your text and make changes or edit your paper instantly without retyping the whole paper.

Here are some helpful guidelines to follow when preparing the final paper. (Your teacher, however, may give you his or her own instructions.) These guidelines can be applied to both a handwritten or typewritten (typed on either a typewriter or a computer) research paper.

1. Use lined paper if you are hand-writing your paper.

2. Use black or blue pen if you are hand-writing your paper.

3. Do not skip lines if you are writing on lined paper. Double-space if you type your paper.

4. Indent one inch for the top, left, right, and bottom margins for both hand-writing and typing.

5. Always indent the beginning of each paragraph.

6. Prepare a title page that includes the title of your paper, your name, the teacher's name, and the date (if your teacher requires a title page).

7. Construct a bibliography.

8. Number each page of your research paper in the upper right-hand corner, beginning with the second page of the body. The first page is not numbered.

9. Organize your paper in this order: title page, outline, body, and bibliography.

10. Do not discard any materials (bibliography cards, note cards, outlines, and drafts) as you may be asked to present these to your teacher.

Sample Handwritten and Typewritten Research Papers

The samples on the following pages represent the final handwritten paper (with marginal information) of student Frank Loftis and the final typewritten paper (with marginal information) of student Tonya Collins.

Title Page

The title page (which may or may not be a required part of your research paper) contains the title of the research paper, the writer's name and, often, the teacher's name, the due date of the paper, and the course name or number.

Title of paper, handwritten and centered on page

The Origin of Greek Mythology

Frank Loftis

Writer's name, centered on page

Teacher's name, course name or number, and date centered on page

Mrs. Annette Haislip

Advanced English

February 3, 1995

Final Outline

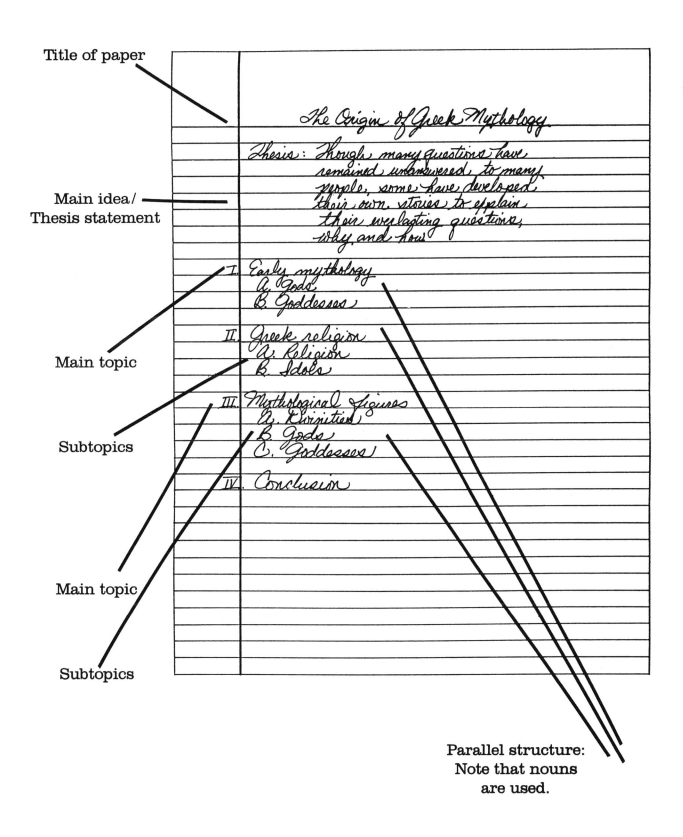

Title of paper

The Origin of Greek Mythology.

Main idea/
Thesis statement

Thesis: Though many questions have remained unanswered, to many people, some have developed their own stories to explain their everlasting questions, why and how

Main topic

I. Early mythology
  A. Gods
  B. Goddesses

Subtopics

II. Greek religion
  A. Religion
  B. Idols

III. Mythological figures
  A. Divinities
  B. Gods
  C. Goddesses

IV. Conclusion

Main topic

Subtopics

Parallel structure:
Note that nouns
are used.

The Body

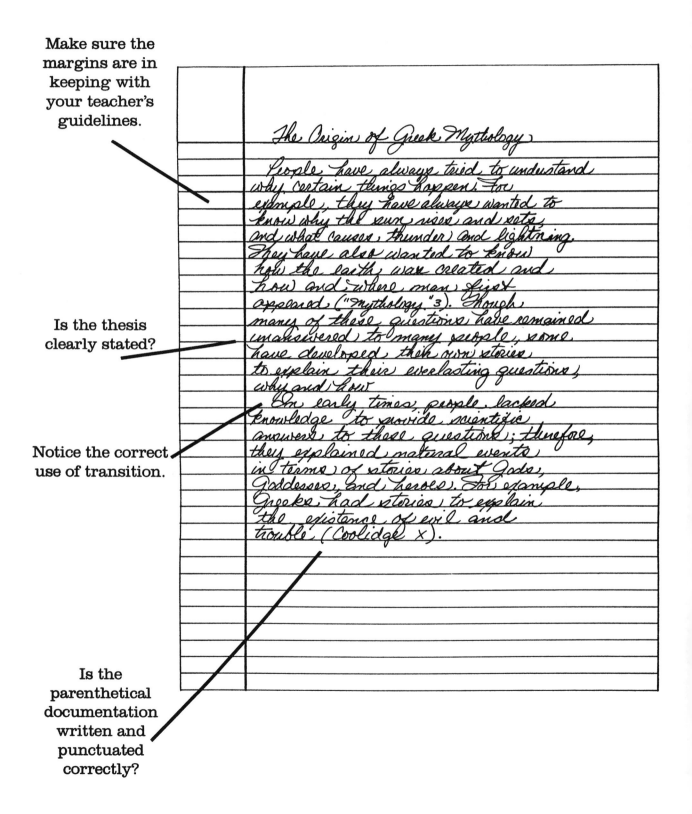

Make sure the margins are in keeping with your teacher's guidelines.

Is the thesis clearly stated?

Notice the correct use of transition.

Is the parenthetical documentation written and punctuated correctly?

The Origin of Greek Mythology

People have always tried to understand why certain things happen. For example, they have always wanted to know why the sun rises and sets, and what causes thunder and lightning. They have also wanted to know how the earth was created and how and where man first appeared ("Mythology" 3). Though many of these questions have remained unanswered to many people, some have developed their own stories to explain their everlasting questions, why and how.

In early times, people lacked knowledge to provide scientific answers to these questions; therefore, they explained natural events in terms of stories about Gods, Goddesses, and heroes. For example, Greeks had stories to explain the existence of evil and trouble (Coolidge x).

Notice sentence
structure and
organization.

Effective
transitional word

Sentence variety
and word choice

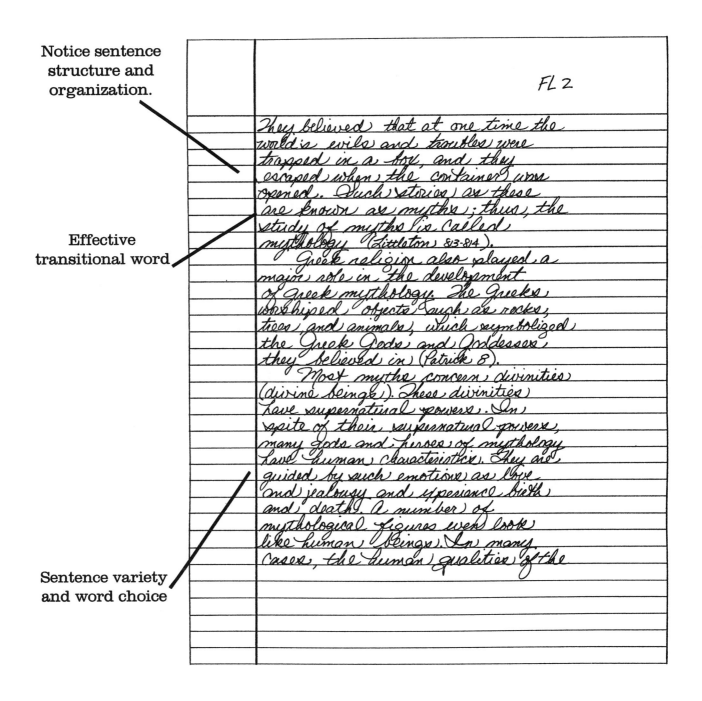

FL 2

They believed that at one time the world's evils and troubles were trapped in a box, and they escaped when the container was opened. Such stories as these are known as myths; thus, the study of myths is called mythology (Littleton 813-814).

Greek religion also played a major role in the development of Greek mythology. The Greeks worshiped objects such as rocks, trees, and animals, which symbolized the Greek Gods and Goddesses they believed in (Patrick 8).

Most myths concern divinities (divine beings). These divinities have supernatural powers. In spite of their supernatural powers, many gods and heroes of mythology have human characteristics. They are guided by such emotions as love and jealousy and experience birth and death. A number of mythological figures even look like human beings. In many cases, the human qualities of the

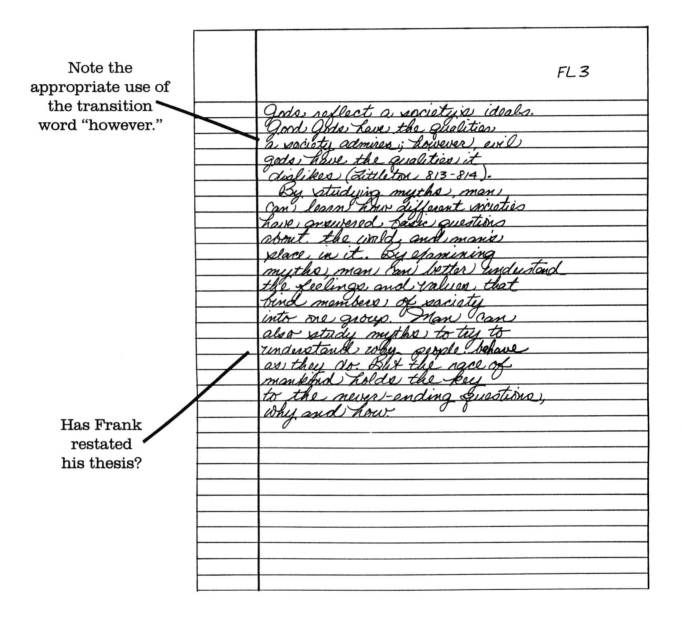

Note the appropriate use of the transition word "however."

FL 3

Gods reflect a society's ideals. Good Gods have the qualities a society admires; however, evil gods have the qualities it dislikes (Littleton 813-814). By studying myths, man can learn how different societies have answered basic questions about the world and man's place in it. By examining myths, man can better understand the feelings and values that bind members of society into one group. Man can also study myths to try to understand why people behave as they do. But the race of mankind holds the key to the never-ending questions, why and how.

Has Frank restated his thesis?

Bibliography

The word "Bibliography" is centered on the last page.

The entries are alphabetized.

Second and third lines are properly indented.

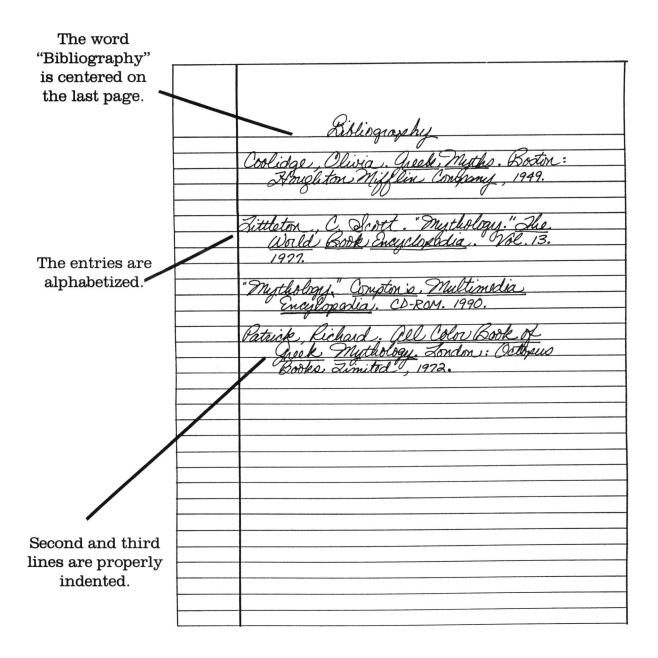

Bibliography

Coolidge, Olivia. *Greek Myths.* Boston:
Houghton Mifflin Company, 1949.

Littleton, C. Scott. "Mythology." *The
World Book Encyclopedia.* Vol. 13.
1977.

"Mythology." *Compton's Multimedia
Encyclopedia.* CD-ROM. 1990.

Patrick, Richard. *All Color Book of
Greek Mythology.* London: Octopus
Books Limited, 1972.

Title Page

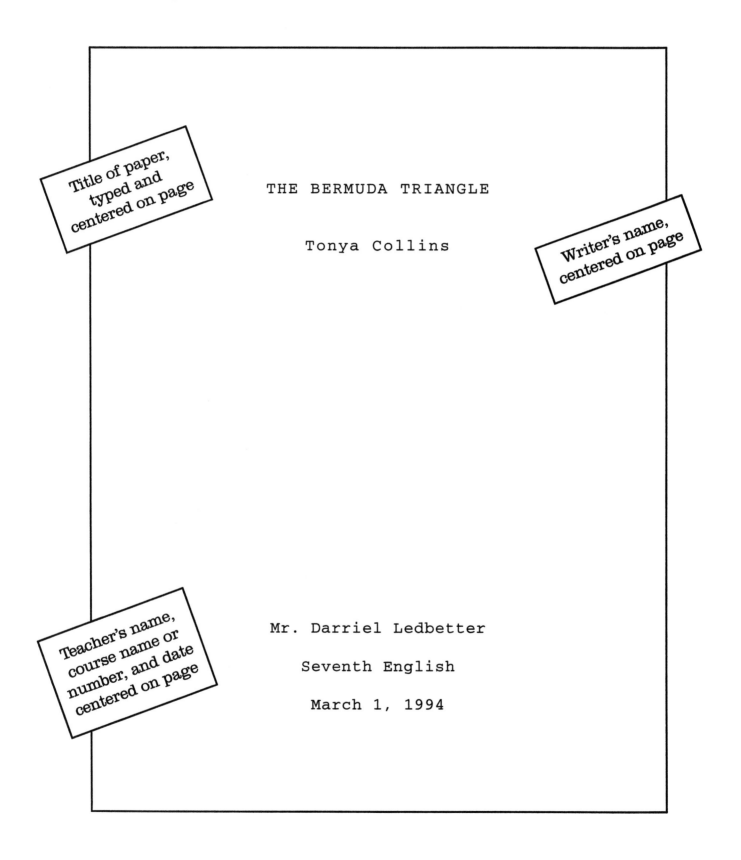

Title of paper, typed and centered on page

THE BERMUDA TRIANGLE

Tonya Collins

Writer's name, centered on page

Teacher's name, course name or number, and date centered on page

Mr. Darriel Ledbetter

Seventh English

March 1, 1994

Final Outline

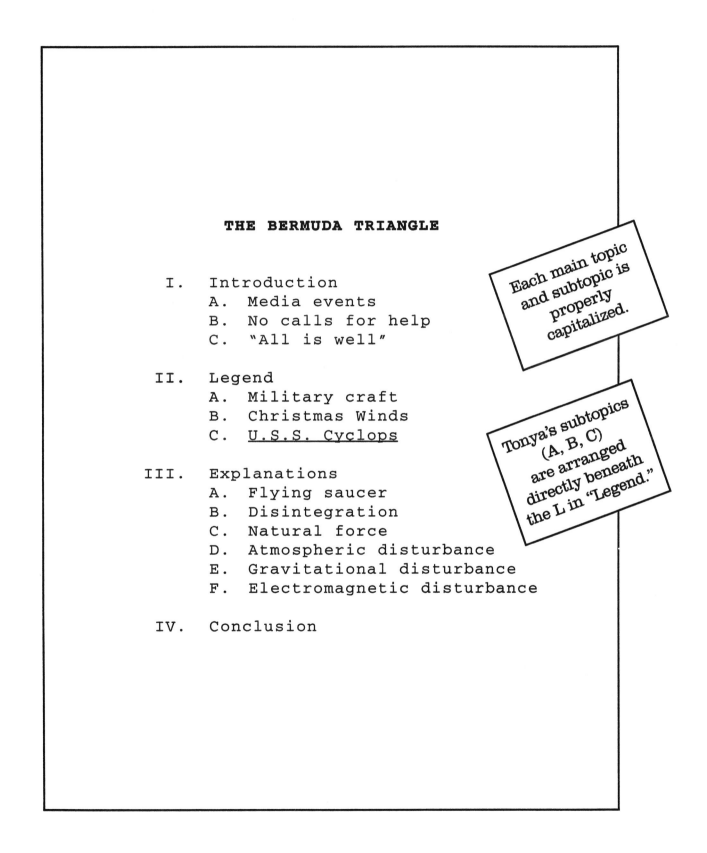

THE BERMUDA TRIANGLE

I.   Introduction
    A. Media events
    B. No calls for help
    C. "All is well"

II. Legend
    A. Military craft
    B. Christmas Winds
    C. <u>U.S.S. Cyclops</u>

III. Explanations
    A. Flying saucer
    B. Disintegration
    C. Natural force
    D. Atmospheric disturbance
    E. Gravitational disturbance
    F. Electromagnetic disturbance

IV. Conclusion

Each main topic and subtopic is properly capitalized.

Tonya's subtopics (A, B, C) are arranged directly beneath the L in "Legend."

The Body

Note the proper use of double-spacing and one-inch margins on both sides of the paper.

Facts and statistics support the topic sentence.

Parenthetical documentation is used correctly.

THE BERMUDA TRIANGLE

The Bermuda Triangle, which has received much attention in the past few years, has been the subject of many books, magazine articles, and radio and television talk shows. A television special was devoted to the Bermuda Triangle. Also, the Triangle figures in the UFO and ancient astronaut mysteries (Kusche 11). According to all accounts, there is something very strange occurring out there.

In this particularly stormy and changeable patch of ocean called the Bermuda Triangle, ship and plane losses can be sudden, surprising, and fatal. Frequently, there are no calls for help, no survivors, no bodies, and no wreckage. A ship may sail into a calm sea under a cloudless sky—then vanish. A plane may disappear there after reporting that "all is well." Some people that have supposedly disappeared in the Triangle have been captured by countries such as Cuba (Cusack 68).

Commercial and military craft cross this area safely every day. Since 1954, more than fifty ships and aircraft have vanished in or near the Bermuda Triangle (Burgress 208). Of the alleged ships and planes lost mysteriously during the last 100 years, most have met misfortune in the months of December and January. During these months, Boreal Blasts and the Christmas

Winds blow across the Triangle, bringing huge swells. Three of the most celebrated victims have disappeared on the same date: December 5 (Gordon 75-79).

The first recorded disappearance of a U.S. ship in the Bermuda Triangle occurred in March, 1918, when the U. S. S. Cyclops vanished. On December 5, 1945, a squadron of five U.S. bombers disappeared, and a seaplane vanished while looking for the aircraft (Burgess 208).

There have been some attempts to explain the Devil's Triangle. Flying saucer enthusiasts insist that everything has been spirited away to outer space. Some say that people from other worlds have completely disintegrated the ships and planes with powerful ray guns. Others believe that everything has been seized by an advanced civilization living somewhere on the ocean floor. Still others believe that the ships and planes disappeared into another dimension (Baumann 110).

The scientists are convinced that some as yet unknown natural force is responsible for the disappearances. The cause may be an atmospheric disturbance, a gravitational disturbance, an electromagnetic disturbance, or something else (Baumann 111). The scientists do not know the answers yet, but they are trying hard to find them.

Until the famous mystery is solved, probably many more strange things will go on out there. Also, until then, many vacationers who plan to take a cruise in the Bahamas will request a ship that bypasses the famous Bermuda Triangle.

Has Tonya properly organized this paragraph?

Note the use of transition.

Bibliography

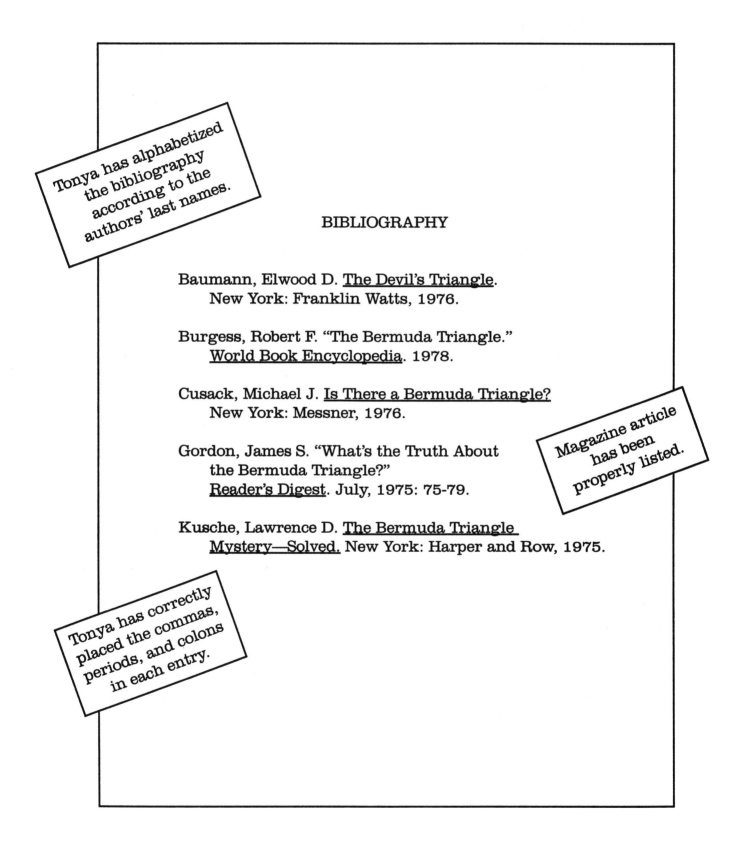

Tonya has alphabetized the bibliography according to the authors' last names.

BIBLIOGRAPHY

Baumann, Elwood D. <u>The Devil's Triangle</u>.
New York: Franklin Watts, 1976.

Burgess, Robert F. "The Bermuda Triangle."
<u>World Book Encyclopedia</u>. 1978.

Cusack, Michael J. <u>Is There a Bermuda Triangle?</u>
New York: Messner, 1976.

Gordon, James S. "What's the Truth About
the Bermuda Triangle?"
<u>Reader's Digest</u>. July, 1975: 75-79.

Magazine article has been properly listed.

Kusche, Lawrence D. <u>The Bermuda Triangle
Mystery—Solved.</u> New York: Harper and Row, 1975.

Tonya has correctly placed the commas, periods, and colons in each entry.

Chapter Eleven

COMPLETING THE FINISHING TOUCHES

After you have finished your paper (handwritten or typed), and before it is ready to be turned in to your teacher, proofread the paper carefully. Remember that YOU ARE TOTALLY RESPONSIBLE for any mistakes in your paper, whether it was handwritten by you, typed by you, or typed by someone else. Before you hand in your paper use these statements as a checklist:

____ 1. I have carefully proofread my entire research paper and made necessary corrections.

____ 2. I have handwritten (in blue or black ink) or typewritten (double-spaced) my paper.

____ 3. I have numbered each page beginning with page 2; I have not numbered the title page, outline page, or the bibliography page.

____ 4. I have read my outline, checking for parallelism, punctuation, alignment, and capitalization.

____ 5. I have checked for misspelled words and incorrect punctuation.

____ 6. I have checked the margins on each page to be sure that they are in accordance with my teacher's directions.

____ 7. I have looked at my paper carefully and made changes to improve word choice (using a thesaurus when appropriate).

____ 8. I have checked my paper for errors in sentence structure as well as parallel structure.

____ 9. I have checked to make sure that my parenthetical documentation (or footnotes or endnotes) is written and punctuated correctly.

____ 10. I have checked for accuracy in my direct quotations and para-phrased material.

____ 11. I have checked for organization and transition in my paragraph development.

____ 12. I have checked my bibliography to make sure that the sources are listed in alphabetical order (according to authors' last names, if given). All the sources used in the text of my paper are listed on the bibliography. Each source is correctly written and punctuated.

EVALUATING THE FINAL PAPER
A Cooperative Learning Activity

Work with a classmate to evaluate each other's final research paper, checking for misspelled words, errors in grammar, incorrect documentation, word choice, punctuation, and errors in capitalization. Answer the following questions as you evaluate each other's paper.

1. Does the research paper have a neat and clean appearance? If not, what improvements do you suggest?

    _____

    _____

2. Do you think the title is appropriate? Why or why not?

    _____

    _____

3. What is one thing you learned from reading your partner's paper?

    _____

    _____

4. Do you think your partner addressed the thesis with enough detail and supporting information?

    _____

    _____

5. Are there any suggestions you can make to improve your partner's paper?

    _____

    _____

6. Does the concluding paragraph restate the thesis sentence? If not, what do you recommend?

    _____

    _____

7. After reading your comments about your partner's paper, will these comments help you in evaluating your own research paper?

    _____

    _____

*Name*_____   *Date* _____

Chapter Twelve

EVALUATING THE RESEARCH PAPER

Name: _____

Title of Research Paper: _____

Content Grade: _____ Mechanics Grade: _____ Total Grade: _____

	Poor	Fair	Good	Excellent
RESEARCH SKILLS				
Use of sources to support thesis				
Use of quotes				
Use of paraphrasing				
Use of citations within text				
Use and variety of sources on bibliography page				
Overall use of research skills				
COMPOSITION SKILLS				
Outline				
Thesis sentence				
Introduction				
Transitional words				
Choice of words				
Organization				
Paragraph development				
Clarity of ideas				
Overall composition skills				

	Poor	Fair	Good	Excellent
MECHANICS				
Sentence structure				
Spelling				
Punctuation				
Grammar usage				
Overall use of mechanics				
MANUSCRIPT FORM				
Title page				
Outline				
First page				
Succeeding pages				
Bibliography				
Neatness				
Overall manuscript form				

COMMENTS: _____

_____

_____

_____

_____

_____

_____

_____

_____

_____

_____

_____

86

CONCLUSION

It is hoped that after "taking on" the research paper, step by step, it no longer seems the fearful and intimidating monster that it once did. You now know the "ins and outs" of the research paper process, and the next time that you are asked to write a research paper, you will probably find the task to be less confusing.

You now also know about the topic you chose to research, and your expertise in this area will most certainly serve you well in the rest of your time in school as well as in your personal life. After all, that is what true learning is all about!

JUST FOR THE TEACHER

The following pages are included "just for the teacher" to assist in a number of ways:
- (1) suggesting research paper topics
- (2) writing parent letters introducing the research paper project
- (3) helping students give oral presentations of their research papers
- (4) providing an achievement certificate

Suggestions for Research Paper Topics:

The following subjects have been successfully used by classroom teachers throughout the country. (Some of these are rather broad subject areas; the student will be responsible for deciding upon an appropriately "narrow" topic.)

- A career in which you are interested

- Earth matters: ecology, endangered species, nuclear waste dumpsites, the greenhouse effect, ozone layer

- Cancer and AIDS

- Influence of other languages on English

- A particular movement in art

- Reflections on short stories (science fiction or Edgar Allen Poe)

- An interesting sport (concentrating on the rules, people involved, country of origin, and how the game is played)

- Space exploration in the United States (early exploration, *Apollo, Challenger*)

- A particular kind of music (pop, classical, jazz, rap, blues, country) from a certain era

- Egyptian Pyramids—why and how they were built

- Death of a friend as discussed in *Bridge to Terabithia*

- Racism as brought out in *Roll of Thunder, Hear My Cry*

- Nature as reflected in the short stories of Jack London

- Revolutionary War period as reflected in *Johnny Tremain*

- Growing up as reflected in *The Adventures of Tom Sawyer*

- Famous mathematicians and their contributions

- Burial customs around the world

- The lives of groups of Mexican Americans and their contributions to our society

- A discussion of the many influences on Mexican music and the different styles represented in Mexican music

- A reflection on the many masterpiece paintings of nature and humanity of Vincent van Gogh

- The influences of Frank Lloyd Wright on architectural principles, philosophies, and designs

- The stock market and its place in our economic system

- The Great Pyramid, a structure causing much puzzlement

- The mysteries of the Bermuda Triangle

- The Navajos: their culture, myths, family life, and language

- A reflection on the many contributions of George Washington Carver

- Sir Isaac Newton: mathematician, physicist, astronomer

- This land is your land . . . America

- The ancient tribes of North America: How did they live? dress? eat? exist?

- The life and work of Dr. Martin Luther King, Jr.

- Harriet Tubman and the "Underground Railroad"

- Earthquake: Why does our earth shake and rattle?

- Isaac Newton's laws of gravity and motion

- Smoking is hazardous to your health

Dear Parents,

Soon your child will begin working on a research paper in my class. Fear not! We will get through this process together. Believe it or not, this is going to be an exciting and rewarding experience for your child.

The research paper is a step-by-step process through which I will carefully guide your child; however, I would like for you also to get involved and become an integral part in this process. You can help by making sure your child visits the library and by questioning and sharing the collected information at home. This research process to which your child will become committed will be useful throughout his or her life—far beyond the walls of our classroom.

Some of the materials that will be needed while completing the research process include:
- dictionary
- thesaurus
- index cards or strips of paper
- pens and pencils
- lined and plain paper
- correction fluid
- folder

As soon as we begin the paper, please check periodically with your child to see how he or she is doing. If I can be of assistance during this research project, please don't hesitate to call me at school.

Thank you for your support and encouragement.

Respectfully,

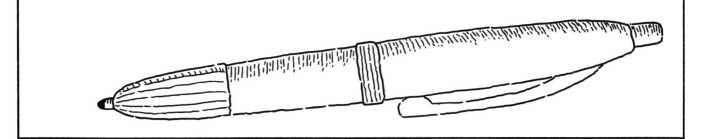

Oral Presentations

After your students have completed writing and editing their research papers, and before they submit their final papers to you, have them prepare oral presentations of their papers. Suggest the following points as they make their presentations:

1. State your research paper topic.

2. Tell why you chose this topic.

3. State the thesis statement or purpose of the paper.

4. Give a brief account of the entire paper.

5. What conclusion(s) did you reach after completing this research?

6. Has this research encouraged or sparked an interest to continue further investigation of your topic?

7. Do not read your paper as your presentation; instead, rely on your prepared notes.

8. Keep your audience in mind by using eye contact.

9. Answer any questions that your classmates may have if your teacher allows the time.

10. Recognize any key sources that were very helpful in writing your paper.

11. Stay within your time limit; practice with a recorder or with a friend.

12. Use audio-visuals (posters, pictures, videos, charts, graphs, records, cassettes, CDs) to enhance your oral presentation.

13. Describe the most interesting part of your research paper.

14. Make suggestions you might offer to a classmate who is about to begin work on a research paper for the first time.

CERTIFICATE
OF
RESEARCH

This is to certify that

_____

has successfully completed the requirements of the research paper

at _____

(school)

Title of paper: _____

_____
Teacher's Signature

_____
Date

INDEX

INDEX

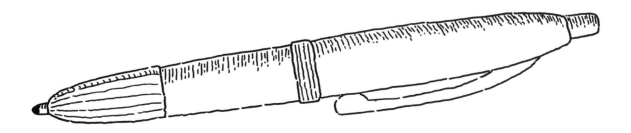